František Palacký (from the *Památník 1898*)

PALACKÝ

The Historian as Scholar and Nationalist

by

JOSEPH FREDERICK ZACEK

State University of New York at Albany

1970

MOUTON

THE HAGUE · PARIS

LIBRARY OF CONGRESS CATALOG CARD NUMBER: 75-114574

Printed in The Netherlands by Mouton & Co., Printers, The Hague.

To my mother and the memory of my father

Otec můj ... býval nad míru přísným, aniž kdy jakou
něžností osvědčoval se k dítkám svým, ačkoli o dobro
jejich ochotně a upřímně se staral; vůle jeho bývala neo-
blomná, často i prchlivá . . . . I matka má byla jediná mezi
tisíci; bylat' čistý obraz neviny, tiché domácnosti a mateřské lásky . . . . Příkoří ode zvášnivělého manžela svého
snášela trpělivě . . . . Literní vzdělanosti neměla naprosto,
aniž rozuměla řeči které, kromě mateřské . . . . Byloť ji
milovati každému, kdokoli ji kdy poznal.

Palacký on his own parents, *Autobiografie* (1823)

PREFACE

In 1876, the year of František Palacký's death, one of his eulogists, Vácslav Vlček, wrote reproachfully:

European science, which with wonderful effort and heroic dedication seeks out the most imperceptible human traces on the whole surface of the earth and in the most remote and inaccessible wastes of ice, sand, and water – that science which, in places long extinct, digs up from the ground with greatest care every potsherd as a memorable relic of human life, and which with the liveliest interest concerns itself about life on the moon and its past – that science for too long [has] acted like a stepmother toward the history of a country situated in the very heart of Europe. ("Dějepisecké dílo Františka Palackého," *Osvěta*, VI, 1876, 402.)

In 1905, Count Francis Lützow could only add sadly that

if one thing is less known than the history of Bohemia it is the life and the works of the historians who have recorded the annals of that country. (*Lectures on the Historians of Bohemia*, London & New York, 1905, v.)

Some sixty years later and after two decades of intensive Cold War-oriented research on East Central Europe, the history and historiography of Bohemia are not significantly better known in the West than they were in the days of Vlček and Lützow.

An excellent example of such neglect is Palacký himself, a figure pre-eminent in both the history and historiography of Bohemia. To most Western historians, he is known only for his important participation in the Revolution of 1848 in the Habsburg Monarchy, a solitary fact that finds its way into most survey treatments of European history in the nineteenth century. Of the rest of his life, especially his central role in Bohemia's great century of national revival, the nineteenth, they know little; and, judging from their manuals on historiography, they are not even aware of the unique place that he occupies in their profession. For Palacký belongs to that enviable band of historians who introduced their countrymen to the technique of modern historical scholarship and who demonstrated it by writing a national historical classic. His contribution to every facet of the historian's craft – to the exploitation of archives, to the collection and publication of source materials, to critical historical method – made him the founder of modern Czech historiography, and the philosophy of Czech history he developed and expounded in his *Dějiny národu českého* made the work not only a monument of learning but also a stirring national manifesto which has inspired the Czechs for more than a century.

It is true that Palacký has received less than his due at Czech hands, as well. Lauded as the "Father of the Nation" (*Otec národa*); his name bestowed liberally on the places and institutions of Czechoslovakia; his every anniversary the occasion for an outpouring of popular eulogy; his home in Prague a museum, his natal cottage in Hodslavice and his gravesite in Lobkovice patriotic shrines; his *History* a treasured symbol of the resistance of Czech to German in two world wars – he is nevertheless still to be the subject of a full-scale scholarly biography, even in the Czech language. Though many authorities in Europe and America have called attention to this serious lack (S. Harrison Thomson, Otakar Odložilík, Hans Kohn, and Arthur J. May in the United States, for example), there are good reasons to account for it. The many important aspects of Palacký's long life and the vast quantity of corresponding source material, primary and secondary, published and unpublished (including thirty-one large cartons of personal manuscript material in Prague, alone!), have made the researching and writing of such a biography a major scholarly task. Moreover, Czech historians have had to do most of their work under restrictions imposed by Habsburg, Nazi, and Communist regimes, all of which have looked upon Palacký as less than a congenial subject.

Czech historians certainly have not neglected their mentor, however, and although much remains to be done, there exists today a large number of scholarly publications on the *Velký Čech*. They have not been synthesized, however, and are largely inaccessible to those who do not read the Czech language. The purpose of this monograph is to present a partial, critical synthesis – a synthesis of the published material on Palacký in his role as historian combined with the results of my own researches into the pertinent primary sources. I hope that it will make a contribution to the history of European historiography and that, combined with a series of other specialized studies of his life and work already completed or contemplated and a thorough archival inventory, it will culminate at last in the long-sought biography.

The first two chapters are introductory – a brief survey of the main figures of Bohemian historiography before Palacký and a biographical sketch of the man. The footnotes to the latter chapter include a critical selection from the vast bibliography on the various other aspects of Palacký's life. The next three chapters deal with his career as an historian and his major historical work. The final one is an evaluation of his influence on the subsequent historiography of his country. Few readers will have ready access to the periodicals in which most of Palacký's works outside of his *History* originally appeared. In citing his major writings, therefore, I have also keyed them to each of the Palacký collections in which they have been reprinted. As frequently as possible, I have let the always-eloquent Palacký speak for himself.

Even as light a vehicle as this must bear a heavy load of indebtedness to others incurred since it was first prepared as a doctoral dissertation at the University of Illinois and an essay for the Certificate of the Institute on East Central Europe at Columbia in 1962. It is the partial product of financial support I have received from the University of Illinois, the Ford Foundation, the John Randolph Haynes and Dora Haynes Foundation, the Joint Committee on Slavic Studies of the American Council of Learned Societies and the Social Science Research Council, and the University of California at Los Angeles. Good counsel, encouragement, and assistance in obtaining materials have come from Professor Ralph T. Fisher, Jr., of the University of Illinois; Professor Peter Brock, of the University of Toronto; Professor Otakar Odložilík, of the University of Pennsylvania; S. Harrison Thomson, Professor Emeritus of the University of Colorado; Dr. Jaromír Loužil and Dr. František Bat'ha of the Literary Archive of the Museum of National Literature in Prague; Doc. Dr. Jan Havránek of Charles University, Prague; Mr. František Palacký, grand-nephew of the historian and curator of the Museum of Four Generations (once Palacký's home) in Prague; and the staff of the National and University Library in Prague. My wife, Dr. Judith Cohen Zacek, has interrupted her own researches often – far too often – to help with typing and editing. To all of these my grateful thanks; of course they do not share in any measure the responsibility for the final result, which remains mine alone.

Albany, New York
August, 1968

JOSEPH FREDERICK ZACEK

CONTENTS

CONTENTS

NOTE ON TRANSLATIONS AND ABBREVIATIONS

TRANSLATIONS

Except where otherwise specified, all translations from foreign languages are my own. Translation of the large number of Czech titles has posed a special problem. To achieve all possible clarity and yet to maintain the continuity of the text and to keep the work from becoming too unwieldy, I have adopted the following scheme: Titles relative to the study of Palacký as historian are listed in the bibliography and have been translated there. Titles bearing on other facets of Palacký's life and those of supplementary works, not listed in the bibliography but appearing in the text and footnotes, have been translated only when it seemed important to do so. In cases of lesser importance, the title has not been translated but the work itself has usually been categorized or described briefly. Titles of Palacký's own works, most of which are not listed in the bibliography, are usually translated or categorized the first time they appear in the text or notes.

ABBREVIATIONS

The following abbreviations are employed throughout this study:

AKBGW	*Abhandlungen der königlichen böhmischen Gesellschaft der Wissenschaften* (Prague)
ČČH	*Český časopis historický* [Czech Historical Journal]
ČČM	*Časopis Českého museum*, generic title for the *Journal of the Bohemian Museum*, founded in 1827 by Palacký as the *Časopis společnosti vlastenského museum v Čechách* and appearing since then under a variety of similar titles
ČMM	*Časopis Matice moravské* [Journal of the Moravian Foundation]
Dílo	J. Charvát, ed., *Dílo Františka Palackého* [The Works of František Palacký] (4 vols.; Prague, 1941)
DNČ	František Palacký, *Dějiny národu českého v Čechách a v Moravě* [History of the Czech Nation in Bohemia and Moravia] (3rd ed.; 5 vols. in 11; Prague, 1876-1878)
DNČ (1939)	František Palacký, *Dějiny národu českého v Čechách a v Moravě*, ed. Miloslav Novotný (15th ed.; 6 vols.; Prague, 1939-1940)
Gedenk.	František Palacký, *Gedenkblätter* (Prague, 1874)
HZ	*Historische Zeitschrift*

JCEA   *Journal of Central European Affairs*

Kor. a záp.   V. J. Nováček, ed., *Františka Palackého korrespondence a zápisky* [František Palacký's Correspondence and Notes] (3 vols.; Prague, 1898-1911)

LAPNP   *Literární archív Památníku národního písemnictví v Praze* [Literary Archive of the Museum of National Literature in Prague]

Památník 1898   V. J. Nováček, ed., *Památník na oslavu stých narozenin Františka Palackého* [Memorial Volume to Commemorate the Centennial of the Birth of František Palacký] (Prague, 1898)

Rad.   František Palacký, *Radhost* (3 vols.; Prague, 1871-1873)

Rodinné listy   K. Stloukal, ed., *Rodinné listy Františka Palackého dceři Marii a zeti F. L. Riegrovi* [Domestic Letters of František Palacký to His Daughter Marie and His Son-in-law F. L. Rieger] (Prague, 1930)

SR   *The Slavonic Review*, since 1928 *The Slavonic and East European Review*

Spisy drobné   B. Rieger, V. J. Nováček, and L. Čech, eds., *Františka Palackého spisy drobné* [The Shorter Works of František Palacký] (3 vols.; Prague, 1898-1902)

ZBG   František Palacký, *Zur böhmischen Geschichtschreibung* (Prague, 1871)

I

BOHEMIAN HISTORIOGRAPHY BEFORE PALACKÝ

> The various periods of Bohemian historiography manifest
> the same peculiar characteristics as the general history of
> the people itself. As the latter presents an almost unbroken
> conflict of political, religious, and national antitheses, a
> struggle for freedom in the face of absolutism in state and
> church, an advance and retreat of overwhelming German
> influences on Slavic soil, so the former could not remain
> unaffected by the respective phases of the fateful contest.
>
> Palacký, *ZBG*, 1.

In Prague, sweltering within its old walls that summer of 1826, the
announcement passed almost unnoticed.[1] The Royal Bohemian Society
of Sciences, at the urging of the learned Abbé Dobrovský and "to
awaken the critical study of the national history among a wider circle
of its contemporaries", had decided to sponsor a scholarly competition.
Sought was a critical evaluation of the Bohemian historians of the past,
from the earliest to Václav Hájek z Libočan. The study was to include
all available biographical information on each author, a collation of all
existent manuscripts and editions of his writings, and a summary ap-
praisal of his professional competence. The deadline for the submission
of entries was set at the end of the following year. The prize for the
winning entry was to be twenty-five ducats and publication of two
hundred and fifty copies at the expense of the Society.

To the latter's disappointment, not a single work had been entered
by December, 1827. Even when the Society magnanimously extended

---

[1] For this sketch of the early Bohemian narrative historians, I have drawn chiefly
upon Francis Lützow's *Lectures on the Historians of Bohemia* (London and New
York, 1905); the sections on historical writing in his *History of Bohemian Literature* (London, 1907); Jaroslav Prokeš, "Literatura dějepisná", in Volume X (*Osvěta*)
(Prague, 1931), pp. 254-305, of the encyclopedia entitled *Československá vlastivěda*;
and references to Bohemia in Josef Šusta's *Dějepisectví: Jeho vývoj v oblasti
vzdělanosti západní ve středověku a době nové* (2nd ed.; Prague, 1946). See also
Palacký's own essay on historical sources in *DNČ*, I¹, 19-37.

the deadline to the end of March, 1829, only one manuscript was ultimately delivered to the secretary. It arrived on the last day, its author's identity disguised, as the rules required, by a pseudonym: "Plus ultra – Nil mortalibus arduum est!" It was duly submitted to the members of the historical section of the Society for their judgment. After months of deliberation, these agreed that "the author of this historico-critical treatise not only has captured masterfully the current state of our knowledge of the subject and presented it in a clear survey, but he has also expanded it with new and important conclusions," and they awarded him the prize. When the announcement was made at the regular session of the Society on December 20, 1829, the author was revealed to be František Palacký, the enthusiastic young savant who had come to the capital from Pressburg (Bratislava) a few years earlier. Published the following year, the *Würdigung der alten böhmischen Geschichtschreiber* remains, over a century later, a classic treatment of early Bohemian historiography and the basis for all subsequent study of the subject.[2]

In the introduction to the *Würdigung*, Palacký was severely critical of his predecessors. Indeed, among their numerous writings he found "not even a single partially-acceptable historical work".[3] The oldest chronicles were fragmentary, full of legend and distortion, and parochial in viewpoint, he charged. "Our old chroniclers were usually private individuals whose insights and sphere of activity were limited; [they were] incapable of comprehending the rich, stirring picture of their times and of describing it for posterity. Their attention was directed either to their immediate neighborhood or to the chief events in the land, whose causes, significance, and results very often remained obscure to them." [4] More recent historians had relied almost exclusively upon these chronicles, largely ignoring the wealth of source materials in domestic

---

[2]   A second German edition appeared in 1869. I have used the Czech translation by Jaroslav Charvát, *Ocenění starých českých dějepisců*, in *Dílo*, I, 63-319. In his footnotes and appendixes, Charvát ably summarizes Czech scholarship on the historians discussed since 1830. The quotations in the previous two paragraphs are from the Society's preface to the *Würdigung*, 67-68. It was apparently composed by Palacký himself! See the draft in his own handwriting in *LAPNP*, Palacký collection, signature 11 C 13.

[3]   *Dílo*, I, 70. The introduction, "Über Geschichtsforschung und Geschichtschreibung in Böhmen", had already appeared under the same title in the Palacký-edited *Monatschrift des vaterländischen Museums in Böhmen*, II (July, 1829), 3-17. See a similar characterization by Palacký of his predecessors in *DNČ*, I¹, Introduction (1848), liv-lv.

[4]   *ZBG*, 16.

and foreign archives. "This explains", declared Palacký, "why even the best Bohemian historians had such an inadequate knowledge of events, why Bohemian history as a whole is composed only of battle scenes and dynastic affairs, ... and why we still do not have a really pragmatic national history edifying to heart and soul." [5] Several years of archival research had convinced him that the systematic use of these long-neglected repositories would give all of Bohemian history a new aspect. "Inexhaustible wells for the historical researcher",[6] they would yield reliable information on the development of the Estates; on legislation and governmental administration; on religion, literature, and art; on industry and commerce; on private and public life; on morals and customs; in short, "information which we still lack so greatly but which today cannot be ignored in the history of any nation".[7]

Palacký divided all previous Bohemian historiography into three periods, each dominated by the work of a major historian: 1100 to 1540 (Cosmas), 1540 to 1760 (Václav Hájek z Libočan), and 1760 to his own day (Gelasius Dobner).[8] The earliest Bohemian historian, Cosmas Pragensis, often called "The Father of Bohemian History" and "The Bohemian Herodotus", was born into a noble family of Bohemia about 1045.[9] He took holy orders, eventually becoming canon and then dean

---

[5] *Dílo*, I, 71. In 1835, writing to his friend, Vinařický, he again complained, "I find too much untruth and even more negligence and lack of discrimination in our old history." Quoted in Václav Chaloupecký, *Fr. Palacký* (Prague, 1912), 130.

[6] *Dílo*, I, 71.

[7] *Ibid.*, 79. Writing near the end of his own career as an historian, forty years later, Palacký attributed the shortcomings of Bohemian historiography in the modern period rather to the opposition and censorship of the Habsburgs. "Without doubt, that government was well aware that its past conduct in Bohemia would not meet with the approval it desired before the judgment-seat of history .... No wonder, then, that it was devoted not to furthering but rather to hindering historical studies." *ZBG*, 2.

[8] To my knowledge, there is no standard periodization of Czech historiography. The following chronological scheme, partially based on the well-known periodization of Benedetto Croce as adapted by Czech historians, may serve: the Chroniclers (to *ca.* 1750, especially Cosmas and Hájek); the Enlightenment Historians (*ca.* 1750-1830, especially Dobner and Dobrovský); the Romantic Historians (*ca.* 1830-1880, especially Palacký); the Scientific or Positivistic Historians (*ca.* 1880-1948, especially Jaroslav Goll and his "school"); and the Marxist Historians (*ca.* 1948 to the present).

[9] In 1903, Cosmas's right to the title of earliest Bohemian historian was challenged by Josef Pekař. In his study, *Nejstarší kronika česká*, Pekař maintained that the chronicle entitled *Vita et passio S. Venceslai et S. Ludmilae* was older, the work of one Kristián (d. 995), brother of the Bohemian duke, Boleslav II. It deals principally with the murder in 929 of St. Wenceslas (Václav), the patron-saint of Bohemia. Pekař's views have not been generally accepted. See Charvát's discussion of the controversy, *Dílo*, I, 318-319.

of the chapter of Prague. His Latin *Chronica Bohemorum*, written when he was already in his sixties or seventies, is divided into three books. The first, from the Deluge to 1037, describes the legendary arrival of the Czechs in Bohemia under their patriarch Čechus, their settlement near the mountain Řip, and the foundation of Prague. Book Two covers the years 1037 to 1092 (to the death of Vratislav II, the first Bohemian ruler to bear the title of king). Book Three, from 1092 to 1125 (the probable date of Cosmas's death), is the most valuable since it includes events in which Cosmas either personally took part or for which he had the testimony of eyewitnesses. Garrulous and shrewd, the author also reveals a nascent Czech self-awareness and distrust of the German neighbor. States his semi-mythical Queen Libuše: "It is more likely that a fish should become warm under the ice, than that a Bohemian should agree with a German." [10]

The many extant manuscripts of Cosmas's chronicle testify to its widespread popularity, as does the number of continuators who successively rewrote it and added the events of their own day, thus extending it well into the fourteenth century. Of the latter, the best known and important in his own right is "So-called Dalimil".[11] Originally identified as a canon of the church of Boleslav, Dalimil is now believed to have been a layman, a noble of northern Bohemia. His chronicle, written in the years immediately preceding his death in 1314, was composed in rhymed verse and in Czech, thus becoming the first historical work in that language. It ranges from the Deluge to the coronation of King John of Luxemburg in 1310. Based on Cosmas for the early period and on first-hand information from 1279 on, the chronicle is nevertheless warped by an intense anti-German bias and is not considered a reliable source. Retorts Dalimil's Prince Ulrich, whose nobles had reproached him for marrying a Czech peasant: "Rather would I entrust myself to a Bohemian peasant-girl than that I should take a German woman as my wife." [12] Needless to say, the bias of Dalimil's chronicle did not interfere with the popularity it enjoyed in Bohemia well into the sixteenth century.

The reign of the Emperor Charles IV (King Charles I of Bohemia)

[10]   Quoted and translated by Lützow, *Historians*, 7.
[11]   This anonymous chronicle was first attributed to Dalimil by Tomáš Pešina z Čechorodu in the seventeenth century. Among the writers especially influenced by Cosmas in the "first historiographical period" Palacký also lists Pulkava (to 1330), Beneš Krabice z Veitmile (to 1374), Vavřinec z Březové (to 1421), "the Czech annalists of the fifteenth century" (to 1527), and Bartoš Písař (to 1530). *Dílo*, I, 72.
[12]   Quoted and translated by Lützow, *Historians*, 16.

was a "golden age" for Bohemian learning, and history was not neglected. Charles himself composed his autobiography, the *Vita Caroli*, an
account of his "vain and foolish life" dedicated to his sons. Dealing
only with the youthful years to 1346, it is disappointing on Bohemian
affairs, in which Charles later developed a warm interest. The *Vita* was
translated into Czech by Přibík Pulkava z Radenína, commonly known
as Pulkava (d. 1380). Taking orders late in life, Pulkava became rector
of the parish of Chudenice and court historian to Charles. At the
latter's order, he composed his own chronicle, from the Tower of Babel
to 1330. Though lacking in originality, it was translated immediately
from the Latin into Czech and thus became the first chronicle written
in Czech prose.[13] Another commissioned work was the Latin chronicle,
in four books covering the period 1283 to 1374, of Beneš Krabice z
Veitmile (d. 1375). Of special interest to Western historians is Beneš's
account of the famous last campaign and death of King John of
Luxemburg at Crécy.

When Charles died in 1378, the Great Schism had already begun in
the West. The European-wide demands for church reform took shape
in Bohemia in the Hussite Revolt, a phenomenon of deep interest for
all subsequent generations of Czechs, not excluding the current Marxists. It is also a period for which many valuable sources no longer exist,
since it became the primary target for Jesuit bookburners after 1620.
Perhaps of greatest value is the *Relatio de Magistri Joannis Hus causa*
written by Petr z Mladoňovic (d. 1451). Until published by Palacký in
the nineteenth century, this source was almost unknown, though brief
excerpts from it, without mention of authorship, found their way into
Protestant martyrologies in various west European languages in the
three previous centuries. Petr was secretary to Lord John of Chlum,
one of the Bohemian nobles sent by the Emperor Sigismund to escort
Hus to Constance. He has left us his "knowledge by eyesight" of the
journey and of Hus's trial, imprisonment, and death – "the last days of
that holy and reverend man, Master John Hus, and his passion which
he meekly endured". This homely, moving account, says Lützow, remains "the foundation of all records of the last days of Hus that can lay
claim to any 'authenticity".[14]

---

[13] Palacký supplemented his discussion of Pulkava in the *Würdigung* with new
data in his article, "O Přibíkovi Pulkavovi z Radenína a jeho kronice české",
Sitzungsberichte der königl. böhm. Gesellschaft der Wissenschaften (1869); reprinted in *Rad.*, II, 471-486; *Spisy drobné*, II, 365-376; *Dílo*, III, 47-60.
[14] *Historians*, 29. Palacký published Petr's narrative in his classic collection of

Of the Hussite Wars that followed, the most valuable contemporary record is that of Vavřinec z Březové (1370-1437?). Vavřinec was a great favorite at the Bohemian court, possibly secretary or chancellor to the king. Appalled by the "vast ruin and the calamities of the once happy and famed Bohemian kingdom", he wrote his Latin *Chronicon* of the years 1414-1421 "that the posterity of the Bohemian race may not lack a record of this terrible ... catastrophe".[15] A moderate, he belabors Taborites as well as Catholics.

Historical studies developed rapidly between the Hussite Wars and the Thirty Years' War. Some writers, stimulated by the late arrival of the humanist tradition in central Europe, turned to describe the stirring events just past. Others took a personal part in the mounting struggle between the Habsburg kings and the Bohemian Estates and recorded their knowledge of various episodes. To the latter group belongs Bartoš Písař (d. 1535). An alderman of Prague, his *Books on the Rising of One against Another, or A Chronicle of the Prague Riot of 1524 [Knihy o pozdvižení jedněch proti druhým čili Kronika o bouři pražké r. 1524]* is a fascinating picture of the demagoguery and intense theological controversy which raged through the towns of sixteenth-century Bohemia. Another of this group, Sixt z Ottersdorfu (d. 1583), was chancellor of Prague in 1546 and wrote of the ineffectual resistance of the Bohemian nobility to the vengeful Ferdinand I in that year (Sixt himself lost his office as a result) – *Akta aneb knihy památné čili historie oněch dvou nepokojných let v Čechách 1546 a 1547* [Documents or Record Books, or the History of Those Two Troubled Years in Bohemia, 1546 and 1547]. But the most promising historians between the wars belonged to

---

Hussite documents, *Documenta Mag. Joannis Hus* (Prague, 1869). Charles University has recently published a new Czech translation, *Petra z Mladoňovic Zpráva o mistru Janu Husovi v Kostnici* (Prague, 1965), and Matthew Spinka has provided a complete English translation, *John Hus at the Council of Constance* (New York, 1966).

[15] Quoted and translated by Lützow, *Historians*, 37. Another valuable source for this period is the group of lesser chroniclers known as "the Czech annalists of the fifteenth century". Often eyewitnesses, they collectively account for the years 1378 to 1527. They were originally published by Palacký as Volume III of the *Scriptores rerum Bohemicarum* (Prague, 1829), under the title *Annales patrio sermone scripti vulgo Pulkavae et Benesii de Hořovic chronicorum continuatores anonymi; Staří letopisové čeští od roku 1378 až do 1527, čili pokračování v kronikách Přibíka Pulkavy a Beneše z Hořovic z rukopisů starých vydané*. The work, edited and annotated by Jaroslav Charvát, is also available as Volume II of the *Dílo*.

a group quite removed from public affairs, the Unity of Czech Brethren (*Unitas fratrum bohemorum*). The order attached great importance to the study of history, the development of the Czech language, and the maintenance of its own archives. Those remnants of the works of two of its historians which survived the Jesuits after 1620 testify to careful research and advanced literary style. Jan Blahoslav (1523-1571), member and ultimately bishop of the community at Mladá Boleslav, composed a famous history of the brotherhood itself, *Historie Bratrská*, of which only fragments remain. Another historian often thought to have been a member of the Brethren, Václav Březan (1550-1619), served the prominent Bohemian house of Rosenberg as historiographer and custodian of the family's archive at Třeboň. Palacký, who himself worked extensively with the Třeboň holdings, considered Březan a genealogist and biographer without peer. The remaining two books of Březan's *Monumenta Rosenbergiaca*, a history of the house in Czech, present an intimate, documented account of the public and private lives of William of Rosenberg, a candidate for the Polish throne against the Emperor Maximilian II in 1574, and his eccentric brother, Peter, the last male representative of the line.

By far the best-known of the inter-war historians (and the ruling figure in Palacký's "second historiographical period") was Václav Hájek z Libočan (d. 1553). From the day of its publication until the nineteenth century, his animated *Kronika česká* [Bohemian Chronicle] enjoyed unabated popularity in Bohemia. Moreover, translated from the Czech into Latin and German it unfortunately became and long remained the primary source for the history of Bohemia abroad. It remained for Palacký, building on the trenchant criticism of Gelasius Dobner, to show that "The Bohemian Livy" was not only an uncritical parrot of Cosmas and Dalimil, but an unscrupulous falsifier and inventor of fact as well, "the grossest detractor from Bohemia's history." (It was Hájek, for example, who originated the much-repeated story that when Jan Žižka, the famous Hussite military chieftain, lay dying, he ordered that his body be flayed after death and thrown to wild beasts and that his skin be used as a drumhead.) "Without any sense of historical truth", wrote Palacký, "he collected a wealth of historical sources, some of them of the greatest value, and assumed that he had sufficiently fulfilled his responsibility as an historian when he reproduced their data according to ... his own fantasy, when he filled ... gaps ... frivolously in the same way. ... With the range of his work as well as the communicative, reassuring tone of his narrative he influenced his successors for two hundred years, with unspeakable damage to history." [16] Hájek was a very ambitious man. Born a Utraquist, he switched to Catholicism early and, after gaining and losing a series of ecclesiastical livings, finally became a canon of the church of St. Vitus in Prague. His chronicle was commissioned by King Ferdinand I. It begins with the Deluge and ends with Ferdinand's coronation in 1526, exhibiting a strong royalist and Catholic bias.

On the fateful Defenestration of Prague in 1618 and the events surrounding the outbreak of the Thirty Years' War, there are several first-hand accounts. One forms part of the *Historie cirkevní* [History of the Church] by Pavel Skála ze Zhoře (1583-1640). A Protestant, Skála held office in Prague under the provisional government and under "The Winter King", Frederick, following that monarch into exile in 1620 and eventually settling in Saxony. There he composed his monumental history, beginning with the conversion of the heathen to Christianity and ending with 1623. Its ten folios, each seventeen hundred pages long, easily earn him the distinction of being the most voluminous historian of Bohemia. One could scarcely find a better eyewitness to the defenestration than Count Vilém Slavata (1572-1652), Lord of Chlum and Košumberk and Lord Chief Justice to the Emperor Ferdinand II, who went tumbling out of the window of the Hradčany castle with his two companions that May day. Slavata apparently felt no compulsion to write about this painful incident until 1636, when his old enemy, Count Thurn, wrote a pamphlet defending the deed. Incensed, Slavata composed his *Paměti* [Memoirs] of the years 1608-1619, basing them on numerous state papers as well as his personal notes. They serve as a prologue to his longwinded (fourteen volumes) *Historické spisování* [Historical Writings], a detailed history of the Habsburg dynasty from 1526 to 1592.

The frightful period in Bohemia after the Protestant defeat in 1620, with its executions and confiscations, its heresy-hunting and book-burning, was not conducive to the writing of history. Some historians, such as Pavel Stránský, joined the mass exodus of the Czech intelligentsia.[17] Those who remained wrote in Latin or German and were careful

---

[16] *Dílo*, I, 74. Of those subsequent historians who were thus influenced, Palacký specifically mentions Pavel Stránský and Bohuslav Balbín. Modern Czech historians have been less harsh in evaluating Hájek. See Charvát's comments, *Dílo*, I, 309-310.
[17] Stránský (1583-1657) published his Latin *Respublica Bojema* in Holland in 1634. Written with great patriotic fervor and dedicated to Rupert and Maurice, the sons of King Frederick, it is actually a small encyclopedia of the Bohemian kingdom.

to placate Church and State. "In general", wrote Palacký in retrospect, "the treatment of Bohemian history was left henceforth only to Catholic ecclesiastics and monks, mostly of the Jesuit order – in what spirit, need scarcely be stated." [18] A rare exception was Bohuslav Balbín (1621-1688) who, though a Jesuit, was of an ancient Bohemian family and could not disguise his sympathy for the Czech nation's plight. It is evident in his rambling encyclopedic compilations – the *Miscellanea historia regni Bohemiae*, the *Epitome rerum Bohemicarum*, and especially in his *Dissertatio apologetica pro lingua slovenica, praecipue bohemica*. The last work was suppressed and published only in 1775, well after his death.

The roots of modern Czech historiography are to be found in Palacký's "third historiographical period." Beginning about the middle of the eighteenth century, it forms part of the broader movement of cultural awakening in Bohemia called the "National Revival" (*Národní obrození*). Both phenomena received important stimulation from the belated arrival of the Enlightenment from the West, especially from France. The rationalism of the movement, encouraging scepticism toward the old authorities, fostered the development of historical criticism. Though Bohemian historians themselves remained largely churchmen, usually members of monastic orders, they increasingly adopted secular criteria for judging the past and, like their French and Flemish counterparts, began to collect, evaluate, and publish historical manuscripts, and to devote their attention to the auxiliary sciences. It is true, of course, that Bohemian historiography was still largely a private affair in the eighteenth century. It was not until 1783, for example, that "universal history" was freed of its connections with geography, heraldry, and literature, and made a required independent subject and given its own chair within the philosophical faculty of the University of Prague.[19] But a rising Bohemian *Landespatriotismus*, provoked by the "Enlightened" attempts of Maria Theresa and Joseph II to centralize and Germanize the Habsburg lands completely, encouraged the Bohemian nobility to patronize the new branch of learning. They began to take better care of their private archives, to open them to researchers, and increasingly to employ archivists and historians personally – not simply to provide

---

[18] *ZBG*, 2-3.
[19] The first incumbent of this chair was Ignác Cornova (1740-1822), a Jesuit-turned-Mason and an important figure of the Bohemian Enlightenment. His chief work was a German translation of Stránský's *Respublica Bojema*, which he continued to his own times.

flattering genealogies and family histories but also to discover historical defenses for the ancient political rights of the Kingdom of Bohemia and the privileges of the Bohemian Estates, both under attack from Vienna. About 1770 they also helped to form in Prague a "Privatgesellschaft zur Aufname der Mathematik, vaterländischen Geschichte, und der Naturgeschichte". Raised in 1790 to the Royal Bohemian Society of Sciences (Königliche böhmische Gesellschaft der Wissenschaften), it occasionally published scholarly works such as Palacký's *Würdigung*, and its *Transactions [Abhandlungen]*, which began publication in 1775, provided a valuable literary outlet for Bohemian historians.[20]

Gelasius Dobner (1719-1790) was a Piarist and a major representative of the Enlightenment in Bohemia. In his many personal friendships, his vast correspondence, his wide historical knowledge, and his penetrating criticism he is rivalled only by Dobrovský. He spent twenty years preparing a critically annotated Latin translation of Hájek's sixteenth-century chronicle (*Wenceslai Hagek a Liboczan Annales*). By 1782 this epochal critique had reached only the year 1198, but it was sufficient to remove Hájek permanently from the ranks of reliable historians (and, many years later, to win the rare and unstinting praise of Palacký for Dobner himself, "this excellent man, the father of real historical research in Bohemia").[21] Ironically, Dobner's intent had not been destructive – he had hoped that his Latin translation of Hájek's work would spread a knowledge of the Bohemian past among a wider reading public abroad. Charged by Bohemian patriots with treason, he replied that it was the duty of a Bohemian historian "for love of country and of science to expunge from Bohemian history everything invented by a later age, and so to save his nation from foreign ridicule".[22] This work, together with a series of critical articles, provided a solid basis for Palacký's own study of the earliest period of Bohemian history, but it was only one of Dobner's projects. His chief ambition was to collect and publish all of the documentary sources for Bohemian history, and by 1785 he had managed to prepare six volumes of his great collection, *Monumenta historica nusquam antehac edita*. For his scholarly service he was awarded the title of "Royal Bohemian Historiographer" and a lifelong annual pension of three hundred florins by the Empress Maria Theresa. In the breadth and depth of his historical labors, he was a

[20] Of the historians of this period, Voigt, Pelcl, Cornova, and Dobrovský were members of the historical section of the Society. Pubička was not.
[21] *ZBG*, 3.
[22] Quoted in Prokeš, *Československá vlastivěda*, X, 262.

very worthy predecessor, if not model, for Palacký. Wrote Rudolf Urbánek: "Today we know that the connection between Dobner and Palacký is even closer than it seemed before, and that the extensive program of historical work which Palacký himself in large part completed and which he then set as the task for future generations finds in many places its prominent predecessor in Dobner." [23]

The survey-history which Dobner did not attempt was accomplished by his Jesuit opponent, František Pubička (1722-1807). Unofficially regarded as "Historiographer of the Bohemian Kingdom", he composed his *Chronologische Geschichte Böhmens unter den Slaven* (10 vols., 1770-1801) at the expense of the Bohemian Estates. Though based on Dobner's documents, the work itself was superficial and did not extend past the Battle of White Mountain. After Pubička's death, the Estates tried repeatedly to have the work continued, but without success. As we shall see, when Palacký was offered both title and task, he managed to convince them that a completely new work was necessary.

Dobner's best pupils were specialists. Mikuláš Adaukt Voigt (1733-1787), a German-speaking Piarist, abandoned his original interest in mathematics and experimental science for numismatics. His three-volume *Beschreibung der bisher bekannten böhmischen Münzen* (1771-1787) earned him the title of "Father of Bohemian Numismatics". As professor of universal history at the University of Vienna, he also catalogued the coin collections of the Habsburgs and wrote on legal and literary history.[24] His fellow pupil, František Martin Pelcl (1734-1801), served as archivist to the Nostic family and is the best representative of the small number of secular historians of this period. With his own pupil, Dobrovský, Pelcl first published the ancient Bohemian chronicles we have so far described, from Cosmas to Beneš Krabice z Veitmile (*Scriptores rerum Bohemicarum*, 2 vols., 1783-1784). His major work, the popular *Kurzgefasste Geschichte der Böhmen von den ältesten bis auf die itzigen Zeiten*, went through four editions between 1774 and 1817, but betrays indifferent scholarship. During most of his life Pelcl wrote in German and pessimistically discounted the future of the Czech language and nation. Toward the end, he changed his mind. He accepted the newly-established chair of Czech language and litera-

---

[23] Rudolf Urbánek, "Palacký-Historik", *Památník Palackého 1926*, ed. Fr. Konvička (Valašské Meziříčí, 1926), 20.
[24] *Effigies virorum eruditorum* (2 vols., 1773-1775); *Acta litteraria Bohemiae et Moraviae* (1774-1783); *Über den Geist der böhmischen Gesetze in den verschiedenen Zeitältern* (1788).

ture at Prague University and started to rewrite his *History* in Czech. Thus his work became the first historical product of the Bohemian Enlightenment in the Czech language.[25]

The culmination of Bohemian historiography before Palacký, the embodiment of the Bohemian Enlightenment, and one of the greatest scholarly figures in all of Czech and Bohemian history, was the Abbé Josef Dobrovský (1753-1829). Goethe himself called him "the arch-master of critical historical research in Bohemia". This erudite ex-Jesuit, his extraordinary critical talent finely honed on Biblical exegesis, was primarily interested in Bohemian literary history and Slavonic philology (of which he is usually considered the founder). His historical production was small. His brilliant study of the murky ninth and tenth centuries in Bohemia, the *Kritische Versuche die ältere böhmische Geschichte von späteren Erdichtungen zu reinigen*, appeared as four separate treatises between 1803 and 1826. He exerted a much greater influence on his contemporaries through his critical editions, reviews, and articles, as well as his wide personal associations. But his greatest contribution to Bohemian historiography lies elsewhere. In 1823, the seventy-year-old patriarch welcomed to his home in Prague the twenty-five-year-old Palacký, fresh from Pressburg. For the last six years of his life, he initiated the eager novice into the secrets of the ancient scripts and sources of Bohemian history. He died in January, 1829, less than a year before Palacký's proud moment at the Society. Thus he was never to know how well his pupil had absorbed his teaching; how he was to combine it with his own unique literary and philosophical gifts; and how, surpassing all of his predecessors, he was to compose a history of Bohemia that would at once be a classic of critical scholarship and a great reservoir of Czech national spirit.[26]

---

[25] Published in three volumes (1791-1796) as the *Nová kronika česká* (New Chronicle of Bohemia), it reached the death of Charles IV. An additional volume extending the narrative to 1429 remained in manuscript.
[26] "Our historians of the Enlightenment are only like John the Baptist, preparing for the arrival of him who was to awaken the historical greatness and glory of our nation from an ages-long spell and to make them the stimulus and guide to a new life, a new greatness, and a future glory – František Palacký." Jaroslav Werstadt, "Politické dějepisectví devatenáctého století a jeho čeští představitelé", *ČČH*, XXVI (1920), 5.

II

PALACKÝ AND THE CZECH NATIONAL REVIVAL:
A BIOGRAPHICAL SKETCH

> If our nation, in the last centuries so deeply fallen, is again
> to be raised even a little, many people must devote them-
> selves to it completely and sincerely without regard for the
> gratitude or ingratitude of the age and persist in the task
> begun, though all effort seem in vain and difficulties in-
> crease rather than diminish. Unfortunately, there are not
> many such people among us, and there is a great abundance
> of work for them on all sides.... Therefore, while I still
> have the strength, I want to assist toward this end....
>
> Palacký to his daughter Marie, January 24, 1851,
> *Rodinné listy*, 63.

The village of Hodslavice lies in northeastern Moravia, where the
Beskyds start their long sweep eastward toward the Carpathians.[1] It
was among these gentle hills that the faith of the Bohemian Brethren
had found secret refuge after the Battle of White Mountain, and it was
not until Joseph II's Patent of Toleration in 1781 that the villagers
abandoned their ancient creed for the closest legal alternative, Lutheran-
ism. No longer forced to worship covertly in the forests, they erected a
church and in 1784 added a school. As schoolmaster they chose Jiří
Palacký, a member of one of the oldest families of the region – and
barely sixteen years old. Though young and meagerly educated, the
new "rector" was industrious. Soon married and in time the father of a
brood of twelve, he eked out his small stipend with a variety of other
occupations: he was a tailor and the local scribe; he tilled his own fields
and sold his produce in Vienna; he even became a *rychtář*, the village
constable. The second of his children, František (born June 14, 1798),

---

[1] Like practically all of the previous "lives" of Palacký, this one is based mainly
on his two autobiographies, composed in 1823 and 1864-5. I have used the editions
of Fr. Krčma in *Dílo*, I, 7-62. Supplementary material is taken chiefly from the
biographies by Václav Chaloupecký and Josef Pekař, both published in Prague in
1912, and from the hoary study by Jaroslav Goll, "František Palacký", *ČČH*, IV
(1898), 211-279.

remembered him as a man who "in all the exigencies of his life govern-
ed and cheered himself with the words of the Bible" and whose penetrating reason and inflexible will were seldom tempered with tenderness,
even toward his own children.[2]

František was a studious child from the very beginning. At the age
of five he had already read the Bible through and was the best, albeit
the youngest of his father's pupils. At Christmas, 1807, he was taken
to nearby Kunwald to learn German. There, in the school founded by
the enlightened Countess Truchsessová, he and his fellows went far
beyond ordinary student fare. But this "pleasant springtime" of the
boy's life ended two years later when his father, fearing the influence of
some of the Catholic instructors, transferred him to an Evangelical
school in Trenčín in Hungary (now Slovakia). The contrast could not
have been greater.[3] Instruction "in the Hungarian fashion" consisted
solely of Latin. Thrown upon his own resources, the boy taught himself
the rudiments of French and Greek and devoured the religious tracts in
which his environment abounded. Soon he began to dream of becoming
a missionary, and only his departure from Trenčín saved him from becoming a religious fanatic. In August, 1812, he left for the Evangelical
lyceum in Pressburg.

Pressburg on the Danube was then one of the most stimulating and
cosmopolitan towns of Hungary.[4] Here German mingled with Slav and
Magyar, and the waning forces of the Enlightenment merged with those
of an incipient Romanticism. Palacký spent more than a decade in
Pressburg, and when he left it the main features of his personality and
life-view were already permanently etched.[5] Here he completed his

---

[2]   Palacký, "Autobiografie (1823)", *Dílo*, I, 11. On Palacký's father, see V. J. Nováček, "Jiří Palacký, otec Františka Palackého", *ČČM*, LXXII (1898), 113-128.
On the Hodslavice environment and the family background, see the two collections
of local studies edited by František Hanzelka: *Sborníček Palackého* (Hodslavice,
1946), and *Palackého rodná obec: Kronika Hodslavic* (Hodslavice, 1948).
[3]   Dagmar Votrubová, however, insists that the cultural level of Trenčín itself
was relatively high at the time of Palacký's stay there and especially rich in the
preserved traditions of the Bohemian Reformation. "Kulturní ovzduší Trenčína v
době příchodu Palackého", *Slovesná věda*, IV (1951), No. 1, pp. 40-41.
[4]   Wrote Palacký, "While the Vienna Congress was still on, I personally saw,
among others ... the Emperor Alexander, ... then Wellington, Talleyrand, and
Metternich, sent by the Congress to the Saxon king in Pressburg; but at the rumor
of Napoleon's departure from Elba, all three returned hastily to Vienna." "Autobiografie (1823)", *Dílo*, I, 18.
[5]   Modern authorities on Palacký seem to agree with this. See, for example,
Jaroslav Goll: "When the twenty-five-year-old Palacký came to Prague [from
Pressburg], he came as a complete person." *ČČH*, IV, 222. Václav Chaloupecký

studies, fashioned his character, and found his life-purpose. The lyceum, says Josef Pekař, "was a small version of the Protestant universities of Germany, already awakened to the romantic national idea and political dreams of liberty".[6] Essentially, it was a five-year *Gymnasium* crowned by a three-year theologico-philosophical school for the training of Evangelical ministers. It enjoyed an excellent reputation, and Palacký attended it with eminent success until 1818. His diploma commends his proficiency in the tenets of the Lutheran religion, pure mathematics, empirical psychology, the Roman classics, Greek and Hebrew, aesthetics, Latin composition, ecclesiastical history, logic, pedagogy, statistics (general and Hungarian), Hungarian public law, metaphysics, "practical theology", physics, and ethics.[7] These studies Palacký supplemented with a broad program of personal reading (he read whatever came to hand – Montesquieu and Madame de Staël; Fichte, Goethe, and Schiller; Addison's *Spectator* and the *Encyclopedia Britannica*) and of self-tutoring in the ancient and modern languages (when he left Pressburg he already knew fourteen of them).[8] His diploma also makes special mention of Palacký's "gentlemanly conduct". No doubt his rigorously moral upbringing was partially responsible for it, but even more so his deep platonic attachment to the Hungarian noblewoman, Nina Zerdahelyi. The guardian of several of his pupils (Palacký added to his meager funds by tutoring) and almost twice his age, she took him into the salons and country houses of the Hungarian gentry, "taught him to live in the world and refined and made firm the manly character

attributes Palacký's interest in Hussitism to the Hodslavice milieu and the influence of Slovak Evangelicalism. Fr. Fajfr and Oldřich Králík locate the roots of Palacký's aesthetic and philosophical views in Pressburg, and Th. Vodička even insists that Palacký changed remarkably little linguistically after his student days. Nevertheless, a comprehensive study of Palacký's makeup in the light of the regional and family influences into which he was born and the intellectual environments in which he received his formal education is still to be made. The only work to deal at length with this period of Palacký's life, Karel Kálal's *Palackého mladá léta (1798-1827)* (Prague, 1925), is a work of moral edification rather than scholarship.
[6] "František Palacký", *ČČH*, XVIII (1912), 269. The Trenčín and Pressburg schools in Palacký's day are described in detail by Jaroslav Vlček, "O škole trenčínské a prešpurské za Palackého mládí", *Památník 1898*, 15-38.
[7] It is reprinted at the end of the "Autobiografie (1823)", *Dílo*, I, 33-34.
[8] Palacký listed them in his diary on January 1, 1820: Czech, German, Latin, Greek, French, English, Italian, Russian, Serbian, Hungarian, Old Church Slavonic, Hebrew, Portuguese, and Polish, as well as the Slovak, Vandal (in Hungary), and Dalmatian dialects. *Kor. a záp.*, I, 58. His proficiency in English stemmed partly from his acquaintance with P. Egan, equerry to Prince Gražatković, whom he met in 1818 and who possessed an excellent French and English library. "Autobiografie (1823)", *Dílo*, I, 31.

in him". It was she who groomed the poor provincial for his lifetime association with the Bohemian nobility.[9]

The new learning and the new environment brought about a religious crisis in young Palacký's life. When it had passed, chiefly through his reading of Kant and the German idealist philosophers, he still believed in a Supreme Power which had created the world and which directed its course through natural laws, in a Christ with divine powers, and in personal immortality; all other dogmas he rejected. The religious zeal of his childhood sought new outlets and found them in a deep, almost puritanical personal morality, in a lasting concern for broad humanitarian issues, and above all in a fervent Czech nationalism.[10]

Like so many of the important events of his life, Palacký's rediscovery of his Czech heritage came about in a dramatic way.[11] In the fall of 1813, the fifteen-year-old was returning on foot from Hodslavice to Pressburg when an appoaching storm induced him to take refuge with an old family friend in Trenčín. The decision probably saved his life. That night the river Váh suddenly overflowed and flooded the entire valley, submerging whole villages, including the inn where Palacký had planned to stay. He was forced to spend a week in Trenčín. His host, a Slovak named Bakoš, took a great interest in the reviving Czech literature and welcomed the opportunity to have the young Moravian translate some troublesome pasages for him. The boy, who had never felt a scholarly interest in his mother tongue, was humiliated to find that he was even less proficient in it than his host. That very evening he began to read Bakoš's books. Once back in Pressburg, he began to study Czech zealously with Professor Jiří Palkovič and assisted him in

---

[9] "Autobiografie (1823)", *Dílo*, I, 25-26. In a valuable study based largely on previously-unused materials in Hungarian, Richard Pražák examines the noble Hungarian milieu with which Palacký became acquainted and conjectures that he may have learned to associate his nationalist aspirations with the aristocratic class through his contacts with the liberal Hungarian middle-nobility. "Palacký a Maďaři před rokem 1848" *ČMM*, LXXVII (1958), Nos. 1-2, pp. 74-99.

[10] Palacký's progressive and undogmatic attitude toward religion is exemplified, for example, by the preference he later stated for the religion of the Czech Brethren before White Mountain (with its stress on practice over dogma) and his statement during his polemic with Constantin Höfler that Christianity needed to develop "even beyond Protestantism". For a professional analysis of Palacký's religious philosophy, see F. Žilka, "Náboženský profil Františka Palackého", *Naše doba*, XLVII (1939/1940), 534-538; F. Hrejsa, *Mladý Frant. Palacký: Jeho vnitřní život a první dvě řeči* (Prague, 1927); Hrejsa, "František Palacký po stránce náboženské", *Reformační sborník*, II (1928), 25-79; and F. M. Bartoš, "Palacký a Augustin Smetana", *Křesťanská revue*, XXIII (1956), 137-139.

[11] The incident is recounted in the "Autobiografie (1823)", *Dílo*, I, 15-17.

the publishing of his Czech weekly and his Czech dictionary.[12] Gradually his interest in the Czech language broadened into an impassioned love of all things Czech. With a trio of young kindred spirits in Pressburg – Jan Benedikti, Jan Kollár, and Pavel Josef Šafařík – he eagerly began to discuss the possibility of a cultural revival of the Czech nation and the role which they might play in it.[13]

Palacký's own future troubled him. "I cannot and do not wish to be a theologian any longer", he wrote to Mme. Zerdahelyi in 1822, "and I loathe dry academic erudition." [14] He first thought of becoming a poet. Since childhood he had assiduously read and written poetry, and his first important published work had dealt with it theoretically.[15] In March, 1818, he and Šafařík had anonymously published their *Počátkové českého básnictví, obzvláště prozódie* [The Beginnings of Czech Poetry, Especially Prosody]. It consisted of six "letters" with accompanying poems, in which the two authors championed a prosodic system based on vowel length (*časomíra*) in place of the prevailing one based on stressed and unstressed syllables (*přízvuk*). It was not only an audacious attack on the older generation of Czech *literati* like Dobrovský, but a fiery appeal for the freeing of Slav culture from German tutelage (German poetry also employed the equivalent of *přízvuk*). After this work, which created something of a sensation in Bohemia at the time, Palacký made plans for others, including a tragedy based on the life of Jan Hus and a grandiose epic on the Napoleonic wars.[16] But as he

---

[12] Palacký's continued diligence in linguistic self-improvement is evident in the manuscript entitled "Slavica: Colligebat Posonii ab anno 1819", which includes many sheets of word lists labelled "Bohemica", "Moravica", and "Slovacica". *LAPNP*, Palacký collection, sign. 11 C 13.

[13] See Otakar Odložilík, "Dni malých začátků", *Husův lid, XV* (1945), 1-10.

[14] *Kor. a záp.*, III, 69.

[15] However, Palacký's first published words, written in reaction to the futile literary controversies of the day, scorned the poet's vocation. In August, 1816, he wrote to Benedikti: "Look at our whole literature. What spaces to be filled! ... Is there not a legion of Czech poets? But where a geographer? Where a naturalist? ... How many historians?" *Kor. a záp.*, II, 8. Benedikti sent the letter to Šafařík, who in turn sent it to be printed in the literary supplement (*Prvotiny pěkných umění*, Nos. 5-6, 1817) to the Czech newspaper in Vienna, Jan Hromádko's *Vídeňské noviny*. A bit later (Nos. 27-28, 1817) Palacký's second publication (his first signed publication), a Czech translation of several songs of Macpherson's *Ossian*, appeared in the same periodical. The latter are reprinted in *Rad.*, I, 434-447.

[16] The *Počátkové* is reprinted in *Spisy drobné*, III, 1-63. The latest edition (Bratislava, 1961) includes a long introduction on the significance of the work for the development of Czech and Slovak poetry by Mikuláš Bakoš (pp. 7-38). See also the discussion by Josef Král in his long study, "O prosodii české", serialized in *Listy filologické*, Vols. XX-XXII (1893-1895). Palacký's other poems have been

gradually discovered that he lacked great poetic talent (his poems, says Pekař, labor with "reasoned rapture, learned mythological apparatus, and strong prosodic concern" [17]), he turned to other fields. A serious student of philosophy and especially preoccupied with the psychology of beauty, he began in 1819 an ambitious *Krásověda* [Aesthetics] in five books. For the first time since Comenius, the Czech language was employed to write a philosophical treatise. But only two books were completed, and by 1823 the project had been definitely abandoned.[18] In that year Palacký took his small savings and left Pressburg for Prague to implement his new, and final plan – to become an historian of Bohemia, especially of the Hussite period.[19]

He arrived in Prague on April 11, 1823. The German cast of the capital shocked him. As he later recalled, "Whoever wore a decent coat did not venture so readily to speak Czech in public places." [20] Nevertheless, he received a warm welcome from a small coterie of Czech scholars led by Dobrovský. Since "strangers of no profession" were

---

collected by Frant. Bačkovský, *Básně P. J. Šafaříka a F. Palackého* (Prague, 1889), and Jan Jakubec, *Básně Fr. Palackého* (Prague, 1898). See also Jakubec, "O básnické činnosti Fr. Palackého", *Památník 1898*, 309-336; and P. M. Haškovec, "Palackého epopea", *ČMM*, LIV (1930), 183-194.

[17] Josef Pekař, *František Palacký* (Prague, 1912), 16-17. In a brief study of Palacký's critiques, published and unpublished, Jaromír Dvořák finds him, ironically, reproaching other poets for the very shortcomings he himself could not avoid – too much description, excessive rationality, too little emotion. "K počátkům literárně kritické činnosti Františka Palackého", *Acta universitatis Palackianae Olomucensis*, Facultas Philosophica II, Philologica I (Prague, 1960), 87-93.

[18] The two books were first published in parts in the periodicals *Krok* (1823) and *ČČM* (1827-1830), then reprinted with other aesthetic fragments in the various collections of Palacký's works: *Rad.*, I, 283-425; *Gedenk.*, 3-18; *Spisy drobné*, III, 64-255; *Dílo*, IV, 91-195. On Palacký the aesthetic philosopher, see Mirko Novák, "Palacký filosof a estetik", *Česká mysl*, XXXIV (1938), 227-245; Otakar Hostinský, "Fr. Palackého esthetické studie, 1816-1821", *Památník 1898*, 367-390; Leander Čech, "Palacký jako aesthetik", *Památník 1898*, 391-442; Jaroslav Ludvíkovský, "Platonsko-stoický prvek v Palackého idei božnosti", *Listy filologické*, LXVIII (1941), 232-241; and Oldřich Králík, "Palackého božné doby", in Frant. Kutnar, ed., *Tři studie o Františku Palackém* (= *Acta universitatis Palackianae Olomucensis*, Vol. I, Olomouc, 1949), 43-165. An attempt to orient Palacký in the general development of Czech philosophy has been made by Milan Machovec, *Fr. Palacký a česká filosofie* (Prague, 1961). Additional sources are given in Chapter V.

[19] Philosophers, as opposed to historians, who have studied Palacký are prone to regard his work in aesthetics not as a mere youthful digression but as a natural, necessary, and deliberate preparation for his transition to historical writing, especially the philosophy of history. See, for example, Králík in *Tři studie* and Jan Patočka, "Filosofie dějin v Palackého 'Krásověde'", *Křesťanská revue*, XXIII (1956), 86-91.

[20] "Autobiografie (1865)", *Dílo*, I, 40.

suspect to the omnipresent police, his friends sought out tutoring positions for him, and Dobrovský himself introduced him to the circles of the enlightened Bohemian nobility. Of these the leaders were the Counts Franz and Kaspar Sternberg. On Dobrovský's recommendation, Palacký was asked to compile their genealogy for Freiherr von Hormayr's *Taschenbuch für die vaterländische Geschichte*.[21] There followed a flood of similar commissions, and shortly afterward Franz Sternberg, himself a talented historical amateur and numismatist, hired Palacký as his personal archivist with an annual income of two hundred florins.

It was through the Sternbergs, too, that Palacký made his entrance into the national life of Bohemia. Late in the evening of December 20, 1825, in the Sternberg palace in the Little Quarter, Dobrovský, the two noblemen, and Palacký sat on after dinner in earnest conversation. Count Kaspar, president of the newly-founded Museum of the Bohemian Kingdom, complained that the institution's rich collections were being ignored by the public. Palacký urged that the Museum place itself in the forefront of the faltering Czech cultural revival, and that it gain publicity by publishing learned journals in Czech and German. When Count Kaspar and Dobrovský remonstrated that it was too late to do anything to revive the Czech nation, the incensed Palacký turned on them, censuring Dobrovský especially for having written almost nothing in the Czech language. As for himself, he said, "Even if I were of gypsy birth and the last of my clan, I should still consider it my duty to strive with all my strength that at least an honorable memory of it might remain in the history of mankind." [22] His listeners were moved, and Franz Sternberg agreed to sponsor the plan for the journals. By the following spring it had been adopted by the Museum and cleared with the police, and Palacký himself was offered and he accepted the post of editor.[23]

---

[21] It appeared in Jahrgang VI (Vienna, 1825). Palacký masterfully characterized his benefactors in *Die Grafen Kaspar und Franz Sternberg und ihr Wirken für die Wissenschaft und Kunst in Böhmen* (Prague, 1843; Czech translation in *Dílo*, III, 283-322). This was combined with the *Leben des Grafen Kaspar Sternberg von ihm selbst beschrieben* and reprinted in 1868 (Czech translation in *Spisy drobné*, III, 412-418, 449-488).

[22] "Autobiografie (1865)", *Dílo*, I, 43. But see Palacký's own pessimistic reflections on the future of the Czech nation which he composed (but did not publish) in 1817: *Spisy drobné*, I, 291-292.

[23] The offer was opportune – in early 1827, fearing that he would not achieve financial security in Prague, Palacký was pressing for appointment as custodian of the court library in Vienna. See the correspondence in P. Váša, "Z neznámé korespondence Frant. Palackého", *Lidové noviny*, December 24, 1927.

The journals began publication in 1827. However, the German *Monatschrift der Gesellschaft des vaterländischen Museums in Böhmen* never developed a wide readership. In 1830 it was reduced to a quarterly, the *Jahrbücher des böhmischen Museums für Natur- und Länderkunde, Geschichte, Kunst und Literatur*, and abandoned the following year. On the other hand, its Czech counterpart, the quarterly *Časopis společnosti vlastenského museum v Čechách*, thrived. As its editor,[24] Palacký was thrown into the midst of Czech literary activity and into the raging battle over Czech vocabulary and orthography, but he refused to side either with the "antiquarians", who clung adamantly to the sixteenth-century usage of the Bohemian Brethren, or with the "innovators", who recklessly absorbed foreign words and coined neologisms. More concerned that the masses "first learn to think in a Czech way and then to speak and write Czech", he closed the journals to all literary polemics.[25] As a result, he was abandoned by many of his resentful collab-, orators and was forced to contribute most of the contents of the early volumes himself. But he persisted, and gradually his contributors returned, coming to include the leading literary and scholarly figures in Bohemia. When Palacký turned over the Czech journal to Šafařík in 1838, it was a well-established national organ.[26]

[24]   Palacký's editorial activities have been carefully studied, especially by J. Hanuš in his long serial articles, "Musejní časopisy za redakce Palackého", and "František Palacký, tvůrce a redaktor časopisů musejních", *ČČM*, XCV-C (1921-1926). See also: Ant. Truhlář, "Z redaktorských příhod Palackého při časopise společnosti vlastenského museum", *Památník 1898*, 290-298; V. E. Mourek, "Palacký jako vydavatel německého časopisu vlasteneckého musea v letech 1827-1831", *Památník 1898*, 269-289; and S. E. Mann, "The Journal of the Czech Museum and František Palacký", *SR*, XXXVI (1957), No. 86, pp. 81-93. Palacký's own writings in connection with the founding and administration of the periodicals are in *Rad.*, I, 5-20; *Gedenk.*, 47-67; and *Spisy drobné*, III, 256-286.
[25]   But Palacký himself became a strong traditionalist in linguistic matters and later took part in the renewed controversies of the 1840's, taking a hard stand against the development of a separate Slovak literary language. See *Spisy drobné*, III, 720-777. Professional analyses of Palacký's own much-admired written style are: František Bílý, "Palacký a spisovný jazyk český", *Památník 1898*, 689-713; and Theod. Vodička, "Fr. Palackého řeč spisovná", *ČMM*, XXV (1901), 1-14, 151-171, 205-267, 369-384. There is an excellent survey of Palacký's progression in linguistic matters from youthful radical to mature conservative by Jaromír Bělič, "Zásady Palackého v otázkách jazykové kultury", in Kutnar ed., *Tři studie*, 166-237. His views on translating (he stressed accuracy of meaning over word for word reproduction) are recorded and discussed by Lumír Klimeš, "K Palackého překladu Dialogu Jana z Rabštejna", *Slovo a slovesnost*, XXII (1961), No. 3, 181-186; and by Jiří Levý, *České theorie překladu* (Prague, 1957), esp. 65-145 and 357-366.
[26]   It has lasted, under a variety of similar titles, to the present day. Selections from Palacký's contributions to it – literary-historical articles and reviews – are to be found in *Rad.*, I, 21-114; and *Spisy drobné*, III, 526-719.

The year 1827 was a notable one for Palacký in other respects, as well. In September of that year he married Terezie Měchurová, the daughter of a wealthy landowner and attorney of Prague. The match further enhanced his contacts with the well-to-do society of the capital [27] and gave him the financial security he needed to pursue his varied interests and programs free of the worries of earning a living.[28] It was in 1827, too, that he was first approached by the Bohemian Estates and offered a position as their Historiographer. Henceforth his official duties were to take up most of his time, but they did not prevent him from playing a major part in the cultural, and later political reawakening of the Czechs in Bohemia (of which his *History of the Czech Nation* was, to be sure, itself an integral part).[29]

"Palacký", wrote Jaroslav Goll, "is a man of many-sided toil, an organizer of work, a man of programs." [30] To Karel Jaromír Erben he declared, "I am interested in everything that concerns the movement and development of the national spirit among us, for we must see to it that it is also a truly cultured and moral spirit. We have a great task before us; without great endeavor, effort, . . . and self-denial, we will not achieve it." [31] An important element of his program of cultural revival was the publication of a Czech encyclopedia.[32] Such a project had long been contemplated and was taken up anew by Palacký in 1829. The work, to be subsidized by pre-paid subscriptions, was to consist of six volumes and to be a concise survey of the contemporary state

[27] These even extended to the members of the exiled Bourbon court who came to Prague after the Revolution of 1830 in France. On the recommendation of Count Chotek, Palacký became for a time (1832-1835) German tutor to Prince Henry, Count of Chambord, grandson of Charles X. "Autobiografie (1865)", *Dílo*, I, 47. Palacký's social position at this time is described in detail by F. L. Rieger, "Za jakých poměrů, zejména sociálních, podnikl Palacký úkol svého života", *Památník 1898*, 45-60.

[28] The delightful mental agonies of Palacký the suitor, based on his own letters and diary, have been charmingly reconstructed by Otakar Josek, "Milostný román Františka Palackého", *Osvěta*, XXXV (1905), 97-110.

[29] Attempts to summarize Palacký's role in the National Revival are the brochures by F. V. Krejčí, *František Palacký, jeho význam v českém probuzení* (Prague, 1912); and J. L. Hromádka, *Palackého osobnost a význam v národním probuzení* (Prague, 1926).

[30] *ČČH*, IV, 211.

[31] Palacký to Erben, December 24, 1844, *LAPNP*, Erben collection, sign. P4AG33.

[32] Palacký's official correspondence on the subject is in *Gedenk.*, 77-83; *Rad.*, I, 225-244, and III, 231-239; *Spisy drobné*, III, 326-338; and *Dílo*, IV, 73-89. See also Rudolf Dvořák, "Snahy Františka Palackého o vydání české encyclopedie", *Památník 1898*, 337-366.

of all branches of knowledge, especially Bohemica and Slavica. A valuable by-product would be the development of a Czech scientific vocabulary. To avoid the Metternich regime's automatic disapproval of innovations, Palacký and his collaborators took the friendly advice of the chief of the Prague police and organized themselves in 1830 as a special committee of the Bohemian Museum. Nevertheless, despite this caution, the project failed, due to fear of the ill-will of the government (which suspected "revolutionary consequences" such as had followed Diderot's *Encyclopédie* in France) and a lack of competent specialists and reference aids. Palacký returned to the project in the 1850's, attempting to calm suspicions by declaring on oath that it had nothing in common with Diderot's. This time the first section was actually completed (in 1852) before the enterprise was again stifled by the reaction of the Bach regime. It remained for Palacký's son-in-law, F. L. Rieger, to publish the first Czech encyclopedia, the *Slovník naučný*, happily, during Palacký's lifetime (11 volumes; Prague, 1860-1874). Though Palacký's plan for an encyclopedia failed, the committee stayed on as the privately-endowed *Matice česká* (Czech Foundation), and despite suspicions on the part of the government that it was a secret society, its membership and financial support grew rapidly. It became one of the centers of Czech cultural aspirations, acting somewhat in the capacity of a literary academy and subsidizing and publishing scholarly works in the Czech language, including such classics of the Revival period as Josef Jungmann's *Slovník česko-německý* (1835-1839) and Pavel Josef Šafařík's *Slovanské starožitnosti* (1837). In 1832 it assumed publication of the Czech journal of the Bohemian Museum and in 1848 of the Czech version of Palacký's *History*.[33] A similar organization, the *Svatobor*, was established with Palacký's help in 1861. Inspired by the case of the celebrated writer, Božena Němcová, who lived and died in heartbreaking poverty, the *Svatobor* was intended to honor the memory of deceased Czech writers and to help support the living. Palacký served as its chairman until 1875.

Still other causes and institutions of the cultural revival of the Czech nation clamored for Palacký's assistance. When he came to Prague, the theaters were a monopoly of the Estates, with the result that "farces and chivalrous plays alternated with pantomimes" and the sophisticated public avoided them. In the 1840's, Palacký joined in requests for a

[33] Official materials on the *Matice* are in *Gedenk.*, 83-93; and *Spisy drobné*, III, 338-349. The history of the institution in Palacký's lifetime has been written by K. Tieftrunk, *Dějiny matice české* (Prague, 1881).

permanent national (Czech) theater and in 1850 was elected chairman of a committee of prominent Czech cultural and political figures organized to head a movement to finance and build it. But the regime frowned upon the enterprise, and in 1852 Palacký himself was forced to resign from the committee. However, he lived to officiate at the laying of the cornerstone of the celebrated *Národní divadlo* in 1868.[34] Throughout his life, Palacký remained a regular participant in the activities of the two leading institutions of the National Revival in Bohemia, the Bohemian Museum and the Royal Bohemian Society of Sciences. He served as administrator of the Museum from 1841 to 1852. During this time, he reoriented it from a cosmopolitan organ of the Bohemian nobility to a Czech national institution and from almost exclusively natural science to literature and history as well. After the events of 1848-1849, the ill-will of the authorities and the fear of his friends prevented his reelection to the governing committee, so that he severed all connections with it in 1852, returning only in 1861.[35] Elected to membership in the Royal Bohemian Society of Sciences in 1830 (to replace the deceased Dobrovský), Palacký served as its secretary from 1840 to 1844 and as its president from 1868 to 1875. Here, too, he helped to revive and Czechicize the institution, using such techniques as having the language accepted for proceedings, creating a section for Czech-Slavonic philology, and pressing for the admission of more Czechs as members (such as Jungmann and Šafařík).[36]

The year 1848 transformed the scholar and organizer of national enterprises into a practicing politician. Palacký's political views and aims are basically clear, though they underwent considerable change and oscillation between 1819 (his first recorded interest in politics) and

---

[34] See Karel Kadlec, "Fr. Palacký a české divadlo v Praze", *Památník 1898*, 473-484. The movement is described in detail in Stanley B. Kimball, *Czech Nationalism: A Study of the National Theatre Movement, 1845-1883* (Urbana, Ill., 1964).
[35] Primary sources on Palacký and the Museum are in *Gedenk.*, 112-127; and *Spisy drobné*, III, 287-325. Palacký's role is also discussed in the standard history of the institution in the Revival period, J. Hanuš, *Národní museum a naše obrození* (2 vols.; Prague, 1921-1923); and more concisely in V. Vojtíšek, "Národní museum a František Palacký", *ČČM*, CXVII-CXIX (1948/1950), 95-103. On Palacký's ejection from the governing committee, see J. Volf, "Vyhazov Palackého z výboru Národního Musea r. 1852 – morální vítězství vlády", *ČČM*, XCIII (1919), 62-63.
[36] See Jiří Beran, "František Palacký jako sekretář Královské české společnosti nauk", in Jiří Beran, ed., *Akademiku Václavu Vojtíškovi k 75. narozeninám* (Prague, 1958), 96-121; and the official history of the Society for this period by Josef Kalousek, *Děje král. české společnosti náuk, s kritickým přehledem publicací jejích z oboru filosofie, historie, a jazykovědy* (Prague, 1885).

his death in 1876.[37] Although he considered himself a liberal and was genuinely concerned with political freedom and constitutionalism, he was never a democrat by conviction. He regarded the franchise not as a "natural right" but as a "political right", to be given only to those qualified to use it wisely. His long association with the Bohemian nobility convinced him that political leadership should naturally remain in their hands and in those of the intelligentsia, which groups could then be safely trusted to look after the interests of the other social strata.[38] What he sought was simply that antiquated feudal rights and distinctions be abolished, that the nobility cease to be "feudal" and become "national" in character. In regard to the political status of Bohemia and the Czech nation and their relationship to the Austrian empire, he was variously a centralist and an autonomist, in favor of a new ethnic federalization of the empire as well as a defender of the "historic rights" (*Staatsrecht, státní právo*) of the Kingdom of Bohemia. Throughout his career and especially after 1848 there is evident a trend toward greater political conservatism and a correspondingly greater commitment to the "historic rights" platform on his part, although full commitment to the latter does not appear until after 1867 (and perhaps not even then).

Before 1848, Palacký played almost no role, of course, in Bohemian political life. As their official Historiographer, he was requested at various times in the 1840's to advise the restive Bohemian Estates on their historic rights and privileges and on the vagaries of the Bohemian constitution. His first significant involvement in the events of 1848 came in early April when, as a prominent Bohemian scholar, he was invited

---

[37] Palacký's political writings and speeches are in *Rad.*, III; *Gedenk.*, 145-313; and *Spisy drobné*, I. Excerpts have been edited by Josef Fischer, *Z politického odkazu Frant. Palackého* (Prague, 1926); and Adolf Srb, *Politické myšlenky Františka Palackého* (Prague, 1898). Summaries and paraphrases are in Fischer, *František Palacký o minulosti pro budoucnost* (Prague, 1926), 48-89. Secondary treatments: Srb, "Politická činnost Frant. Palackého", *Památník 1898*, 545-601; Rudolf Wierer, "F. Palacký's staatspolitisches Programm", *Zeitschrift für Ostforschung*, VI (1957), 246-258; I. Udal'tsov, "K charakteristike politickej činnosti Františka Palackého", *Historický sborník Slovenskej akadémie vied a umení*, X (1952), 347-369 (translated and reprinted from *Voprosy istorii*, 1950, No. 10, 72-85); and especially Fischer, *Myšlenka a dílo Františka Palackého* (2 vols.; Prague, 1926-1927), I, 207-285, II, 262-362, where Palacký's political ideas and their philosophical origins are analyzed in detail.

[38] Palacký's rather conservative social views are described and sharply criticized from a Marxist point of view by Bedřich Šindelář, "František Palacký a dělnická třída", *ČMM*, LXXI (1952), 19-40; and Milena Jetmarová, "K hodnocení společenských názorů Palackého před rokem 1848", *Filosofický časopis*, IV (1956), 843-864, largely repeated in her book, *František Palacký* (Prague, 1961), 17-52.

to become one of the Committee of Fifty preparing for the All-German Constituent Assembly in Frankfurt. He replied on April 11 with his celebrated letter of refusal:

I am not a German .... I am a Czech of Slavonic blood. ... [My] nation is a small one, it is true, but from time immemorial it has been a nation of itself and existing of itself. ... The entire connection of the Czech lands with the German Reich ... must be regarded not as a bond between nation and nation but as one between ruler and ruler. ... It is your irrevocable desire and purpose to undermine Austria as an independent empire and indeed to make her impossible for all time to come – an empire whose preservation, integrity, and consolidation is, and must be, a great and important matter not only for my own nation but also for the whole of Europe, indeed, for humanity and civilization itself. ... You know that [Russia], now grown to vast dimensions, increases in strength ... decade by decade. ... The bare possibility of a universal Russian monarchy has no more determined opponent or foe than myself. ... You know that in Southeast Europe, along the frontier of the Russian Empire, there live many nations, ... none of whom is sufficiently powerful itself to successfully defy its superior neighbor on the east. ... They could do so only if a close and firm tie bound them all together as one. ... Assuredly, if the Austrian State had not existed for ages, in the interests of Europe and indeed of humanity itself we would have to endeavor to create it as soon as possible. ... By nature and history [it is] summoned to be the bulwark and guardian of Europe against Asiatic elements of every sort. ... The fundamental rule [must be] that all the nationalities and all the religions under her scepter should enjoy complete equality of rights and respect in common. ... If Europe is to be saved, Vienna must not sink to the role of a provincial town.[39]

The letter made Europeans (and doubtless a great many Czechs, too) suddenly and strikingly aware of the existence of a Czech nation. Palacký himself was convinced that it had materially helped to save the Habsburg empire in 1848.[40]

Soon afterward, at the beginning of June, he was elected chairman of the Slavonic Congress which met in Prague as a counterweight to the Frankfurt Asembly and there reaffirmed the loyalty of the Austro-Slavs

[39] A Czech version of this much-translated letter is in *Spisy drobné*, I, 16-22; a German one in *Gedenk.*, 149-155; an English one by William Beardmore in *SR*, XXVI (1947/1948), 303-308.
[40] On April 16, 1848, Palacký wrote to Šafařik that he had received "still another letter from Frankfurt, a very flattering one, almost pleading, stating that the Germans are willing to give necessary guarantees to the Czechoslovak nationality, that my arrival there will occasion general rejoicing, etc., etc. – 'The whistle sounds sweetly, when the fowler lures the birds'." V. Bechyňová and Z. Hauptová, eds., *Korespondence P. J. Šafaříka s F. Palackým* (Prague, 1961), 192. In gratitude for Palacký's reassuring Austroslavism, Vienna twice (May 8, September 2) offered him the portfolio of Imperial Minister of Public Instruction, which he refused in order to avoid alienating the Germans in the empire.

to the empire.[41] Meanwhile, he had also become a member of the national committee charged with preparing the draft of a constitution for the discussion of a forthcoming constituent assembly in Bohemia, and part of the eight-member provisional executive council established under the new governor, Count Thun, to help him administer the kingdom. All of these promising activities were cut short by the riots of students and workers in Prague in mid-June, when the country was placed under martial law. All hope now lay in the Imperial Constituent Assembly which opened in July in Vienna (moving in October to Kremsier in Moravia). As a member of the committee charged with drafting a constitution for the empire, Palacký submitted two plans, the second of which proposed a federalistic arrangement in which political power would be shared between eight equal national (ethnic) divisions and a central government in Vienna. The plan, often referred to subsequently as one which might have preserved the viability of the multi-national empire, was rejected, and Palacký resigned from the committee.[42] Soon afterward, in March, 1849, the Kremsier parliament itself was dissolved.

From 1851, when open absolutism was reimposed, to 1860 Palacký was, in his own words, "exiled from the press of national life". He was placed under police surveillance and the threat of imprisonment, the Bohemian Estates denounced him for his reluctance to defend their inherited rights, and many of his friends were frightened away. He wrote to his son in 1853: "I do not know what future awaits us, but I know what my duty is: to endure with the nation to the last breath, to strive in every possible way for its good, and all the while to be as careful as a snake and as innocent as a dove." [43] He spent most of the period in retirement with his family on his estate in Lobkovice, engaged mainly in writing his *History*, an activity ultimately far more dangerous to the

[41] See also Václav L. Beneš, "Bakunin and Palacký's Concept of Austroslavism", *Indiana Slavic Studies*, II (1958), 79-111.
[42] The two drafts (September, 1848, and January, 1849) are translated into Czech in *Spisy drobné*, I, 57-64, 68-74; the first, in German, is in *Gedenk.*, 169-176; see also Palacký's exegesis of the second in *Spisy drobné*, I, 75-90. A "third draft", similar to the second but more anti-centralistic, appeared in Palacký's article, "O centralisaci a národní rovnoprávnosti v Rakousku", in Karel Havlíček's *Národní noviny*, December 21, 1849 (Czech versions in *Spisy drobné*, I, 110-120, and *Rad.*, III, 59-70; German version in *Gedenk.*, 206-214). See also Frant. Kameníček, *František Palacký v ústavním výboru říšského sněmu rakouského (1848-1849)* (Prague, 1929); Bohuš Rieger, "Ústava Rakouska dle Frant. Palackého v l. 1848-49", *Památník 1898*, 602-645; and Otakar Odložilík, "A Czech Plan for a Danubian Federation – 1848", *JCEA*, I (1941/1942), 253-274.
[43] Palacký to Jan Palacký, March 7, 1853, in Čeněk Zíbrt, ed., "Z dopisů Františka Palackého synu Janovi", *Osvěta*, XXXIX (1909), 50.

fortunes of the multi-national empire than anything he had done or would do as a politician.

With the resumption of constitutional life in 1860, Palacký returned to modest political activity. Named a life member of the House of Lords of the Imperial Diet in April, 1861, he attended it only briefly and, finding himself isolated and ineffectual, abandoned it permanently in September of the same year. He also returned to the Bohemian Diet in 1861, and until his death he and his son-in-law, František L. Rieger, were the recognized leaders of the National Party ("Old Czechs"). As such, he effected a rapprochement with the conservative nobility and later, after the Austro-Hungarian Compromise, supported the "passive resistance" of the Czech delegates to both diets. In 1865 he published his altered political views in his *Idea státu rakouského* [The Idea of the Austrian State], in which he reworked his federal program of 1848-1849 on the basis of historical-territorial entities and "historic rights", warning against centralism and impending dualism in the empire with the words, "We existed before Austria, we shall still exist when it is gone." [44] When in 1867 dualism was actually proclaimed, he led a disillusioned Czech delegation in protest to the All-Slav Ethnographic Exhibition in Moscow.

In the 1870's, his health failing, Palacký withdrew from direct political activity, hurrying to complete his *History* and to prepare a series of memoirs in which he reviewed and justified his past ideas and acts and stated his counsels and expectations for the future.[45] In them he characterized as a great error his attempt to maintain a strong, united Austrian empire and to obtain justice for the Czech nation from its German rulers and fellow inhabitants. That justice, he now prophesied, would ultimately be obtained through a great war ("a great conflagration, a new Thirty Years' War") in which Germany, seeking European hegemony, would be defeated by a coalition of eastern and western

---

[44] The *Idea* is reprinted in *Rad.*, III, 158-230; and *Spisy drobné*, I, 209-267; German version, *Österreichs Staatsidee* (Prague, 1866).

[45] Chief among these are the epilogues to the collections *Radhost* (1872) and *Gedenkblätter* (1874), reprinted in *Spisy drobné*, I, 334-371, 390-411, and III, 778-791. The former has also been reprinted as *Palacký's politisches Vermächtniss* (Prague, 1872) and *Fr. Palacký: Poslední mé slovo* (Prague, 1912); the latter as *Fr. Palackého nejnovější politické úvahy* (Prague, 1874). They have been reprinted together as *Fr. Palacký: Poslední slova*, ed. J. Borovička (Prague, 1917), and as Palacký's "political testament" – *Politická závěť Františka Palackého*, ed. Jar. Werstadt (Prague, 1928). See also Werstadt's summary, *Palackého odkaz potomstvu a osvobozenému národu* (Prague, 1926), reprinted in his *Odkazy dějin a dějepisců* (Prague, 1948), 43-64.

powers. Meanwhile, he turned hopefully to the promise of all-Slav solidarity, to the help and friendship of a benign France and a politically liberalized Russia,[46] and especially to the continuing moral and cultural development of the Czechs themselves:

Whenever we were victorious, it was always due rather to spiritual superiority than to physical might, and whenever we succumbed it was always the fault of a lack of spiritual activity and moral courage. . . . If we do not raise our spirit and the spirit of our nation to higher and more noble activity than our neighbors, not only will we fail to achieve an honorable place in the ranks of nations, but we will not succeed in defending finally even our original home.[47]

And if all our patriots will work in a sincere and cultivated way, then I have no fear for our nationality and our nation. It will maintain itself as long as it wishes and longer than its enemies wish.[48]

Thus the moralist and scholar again supplanted the politician and supplied the answer which the latter had sought and failed to find.

Palacký's last years passed quietly, disturbed only by a triumphant, emotional journey to his birthplace, Hodslavice, in 1873,[49] and a gala celebration of the completion of his *History* in Prague on April 23, 1876. He died on May 26, 1876, of dropsy, and was buried in Lobkovice, laden with honors and mourned as the "Father of the Nation". "His funeral", says his biographer, Václav Chaloupecký, "was greater than that of a king." [50]

[46]   On the growth of Palacký's "Slavophilism" and "Russophilism", see Jan Slavík, "Palackého cesta k rusofilství", in František Hanzelka, ed., *Sborníček Palackého 1946* (Hodslavice, 1946), 20-24; František Kutnar, "Palackého slovanství", *Slovanský přehled*, XLII (1956), 153-154; and Václav Čejchan, "Rusofilství Františka Palackého po r. 1848", *Slovanský přehled*, LII (1966), 1-5.
[47]   "Speech at the General Meeting of Svatobor, November 27, 1864", in *Spisy drobné*, I, 205-6.
[48]   "Speech at the Commemorative Banquet of April 23, 1876", in *Spisy drobné*, I, 427.
[49]   The moving last journey through Moravia is described in detail by Fr. Bayer and Fr. Koželuha, *Fr. Palackého poslední loučení s rodnou Moravěnkou r. 1873* (Přerov, 1898).
[50]   *František Palacký*, 188. Among his distinctions were honorary citizenship in more than a thousand cities and towns of Bohemia and Moravia and membership in several dozen foreign academies and learned societies, including the Hungarian Learned Society in Pest, the Royal Bavarian Academy of Sciences in Munich, the Royal Prussian Academy of Sciences in Berlin, the Imperial Academy of Sciences in Vienna, the Society for the History and Antiquities of the South Slavs in Zagreb, and the Imperial Academy of Sciences in St. Petersburg. Among his decorations were the Austrian Order of the Iron Crown (Second Class), awarded to him in 1866 by Emperor Franz Josef I, "in recognition of his services to learning and especially to Bohemian historiography". *ZBG*, 144. Details of his will, by which he left the major part of his papers and manuscripts to the Bohemian Museum, are given by Josef Vejvara, "Soudní projednání pozůstalosti po historiografu Frant. Palackém", *ČČM*, LXXXIII (1910), 136-145.

III

THE PREPARATORY LABORS

> I might complain that in Bohemia I alone have been bur-
> dened with work which in other countries is shared by
> governments, academies, and educational institutions; that
> I not only have to make my own way in so many spheres
> from beginning to end, but that I myself must also travel
> about the whole world in search of sources and be my own
> copyist; that at the same time I must be hod-carrier and
> master-builder in one person.
> Palacký to Count Chotek, February 24, 1842, *ZBG*, 90.

The earliest solid evidence we possess that young Palacký's interests
were turning from poetry and philosophy to history is contained in a
letter he wrote from Pressburg in December, 1818, to Josef Jungmann,
the prominent Czech writer in Prague. In it he stated his intention to
write, among other works, "a history of Bohemia in the fifteenth century – à la Robertson", expressed his eagerness to study in Prague, and
queried his friend about the possibility of earning a livelihood there.[1]
The plan was apparently more than a passing whim. When his three
friends – Benedikti, Kollár, and Šafařík – returned to Pressburg from
the University of Jena in the summer of 1819, he eagerly laid it before
them.[2] Their response was not enthusiastic. Benedikti even held that
"the Czechs could not have a great historian because they do not have
a great history". Palacký countered with the examples of the Scot,
Robertson, and the Swiss, Müller, and maintained that despite great
handicaps – their small numbers, their landlocked geographical position,

---

[1] Palacký to Jungmann, December 3, 1818, *Kor. a záp.*, III, 30. After a very careful study of the available evidence, especially Palacký's correspondence and personal
notes, Králík (in Kutnar, ed., *Tři studie*, 153-155) has also chosen 1818 as the year
when Palacký turned to history, especially the history of the Hussites.
[2] The incident is reported in Palacký's "Každodenníček" [Diary], in the undated
entry covering the period from April 14 to the beginning of July, 1819. *Kor a záp.*,
I, 34-36.

the enmity of their German neighbors, and their domestic upheavals – the Czechs had had a noteworthy past:

The glory of nations is not based on their number or on their physical strength: it lies in their life, their spirit [duch]. Only that nation is worthy of living on in the annals of mankind which has lived as a nation, not as an aggregate of individual or servile human animals. The spirit of a nation appears there, where with all its goods it is ready to live and die for an idea.[3]

When Benedikti continued that even if there had been some glorious moments in the Czech past they could no longer be accurately conceived in their true historical spirit because that spirit had died out in Bohemia, "and only through life can life be understood," Palacký replied that an enthusiastic and imaginative historian needed only the musty chronicles from which to recreate "history as it was" ("dějiny tak jak byly").

If his friends brought discouragement, they also provided its antidote. At Jena they had heard the stirring lectures of the nationalistic German historian, Heinrich Luden, and these they now retailed to Palacký. He was especially impressed with Luden's thesis that the way to true patriotism and to national unity lay in the knowledge of the "spirit" of one's people as revealed in their history:

The more strongly the spirit of his nation [Volk] lives and works [in a man], the more deeply true love of his fatherland animates him, the more earnestly he will study the history of his nation, because he will wish to see and to understand the spirit of his nation. ... And he will wish to know this and must know this in order to be able to live and work for his nation on firm principles. ... In human life there is only one way to an understanding of the present – the way through the past. That is the special, unique value which ... the history of one's fatherland has, which all history affords. ... Indeed, every nation, which endured as such and arrived at a unified culture, which possessed unity and individuality, has also studied its own history with manifold interest; every man who truly belonged to a nation, who had a fatherland or was worthy of having one, has always loved history, above all the history of his nation.[4]

---

[3] Ibid., 36.
[4] Luden, Einige Wörte über das Studium der vaterländischen Geschichte: Vier öffentliche Vorlesungen aus dem Jahre 1808 (Jena, 1810), 18-19, quoted in Richard Georg Plaschka, Von Palacký bis Pekař (Graz-Köln, 1955), 6. At this time Palacký apparently knew Luden's teachings only from the accounts of his friends. Although there is a vague reference in his diary to his having read "Luden" among others in the summer of 1819 (Kor. a záp., I, 35 – apparently a copy of Luden's periodical, Nemesis: Zeitschrift für Politik und Geschichte), it was not until February 19, 1826, that he recorded: "I read for the first time Luden's German history" ("Každodenníček", Kor. a záp., I, 136 – Luden's Geschichte des teutschen Volkes, of which the

This idea, repeated in other works such as L. Jahn's *Das deutsche Volksthum* and Karamzin's *Istoriia gosudarstva rossiiskago*, convinced him that in history he had made a wise choice, not only of a vocation but of a means of contributing to the Czech national revival. Here was the way to reconcile those literary and nationalist aspirations which competed perpetually within him.

Thus reassured, Palacký settled down to serious preparation. That very summer he began an intensive reading program, writing again to Jungmann for advice: Was there a printed collection of all documents pertaining to Bohemian history? What was the most complete and critical history of Bohemia extant? Which authors and what manner of study would Jungmann recommend? [5] On the eve of 1820, as part of an elaborate balance sheet of his life, he recorded in his diary as one of the "goals of his life" "a pragmatic history of the land of Bohemia, according to the ideals of historical art".[6] Two years later, he wrote to Kollár: "I am completely immersed now in histories; I cannot live if I cannot devote myself to our national history. At least the Hussite period ... I will surely write." [7] By early 1823 he had resolved to continue his historical studies in Prague. In March, a month before his arrival in the capital, he wrote of his decision to Dobrovský, whom he had met in 1820 during a visit to Vienna: "It is my purpose to devote myself [in Prague] chiefly to the study of the sources of Bohemian history, for long ago I made the irrevocable resolution to dedicate my life completely to our national history if external circumstances would only in some measure permit it. In any case, I shall try to maintain myself [there] for at least two years: but my greatest wish is that I might have the prospect of spending my whole future life there, amid the monuments of our national history." [8]

Before he left Pressburg, Palacký's historical training consisted entirely of personal reading. An examination of the titles and excerpts

---

first volume appeared in 1825). Several of Benedikti's letters to Palacký mention Luden, e.g., the one of August 18, 1817: "If you heard the latter [Luden] ... when, as if inspired by a higher spirit, he speaks of love for his German fatherland, of freedom for his dear nation, I think you would be pierced and inflamed with love for your own nation." *Kor. a záp.*, III, 18. Luden's activities at Jena and his historical and nationalistic theories are described in the printed doctoral dissertation by Johannes Haage, *Heinrich Luden: Seine Persönlichkeit und seine Geschichtsauffassung* (Leipzig, 1930?).

5   Palacký to Jungmann, July 14, 1819, *Kor. a záp.*, III, 36.
6   "Každodenníček", *Kor. a záp.*, I, 62.
7   Palacký to Kollár, August, 1822, *Kor. a záp.*, II, 99.
8   Palacký to Dobrovský, March 3, 1823, *ibid.*, III, 74.

recorded in his diary[9] shows that it was haphazard and of uneven quality. It included almost no study of original sources and few of the basic contemporary works on history in general and Bohemian history in particular. The chronicles of Dalimil and Hájek he already knew from his work with Palkovič, and Pelcl's *Nová kronika česká* was the first work he purchased on Bohemian history (1814). He also read Johannes Müller's *Geschichte der schweizerischen Eidgenossenschaft,* Karamzin's *Istoriia gosudarstva rossiiskago,* Gibbon's *Decline and Fall,* William Robertson's *History of Scotland,* Lenfant's *Histoire de la guerre des Hussites,* David Cranz's *Alte und neue Brüderhistorie,* and Dobrovský's *Geschichte der böhmischen Sprache und Literatur.*[10] As Pekař has pointed out, "Palacký's historical preparation in general began where today the training of an historian culminates or more often fails to arrive" – in historical method and style, and in the philosophy of history.[11] In those spheres he was relatively advanced, thanks to his regular reading of literary reviews and the works of several outstanding English and German authors, including Hugh Blair, Bolingbroke, Luden, Kant, Hegel, and Herder. Indeed, leading authorities agree that Palacký's views on the theory and philosophy of history, notably his commitment to the ideals of impartiality and objectivity and to the "eternal law of polarity" as the mainspring of history, were essentially formed before he left Pressburg and changed little thereafter.

 Palacký was also aware of the historian's primary responsibility to

---

[9] The very idea of including such excerpts in a diary Palacký derived from reading a similar work by a famous historian, Gibbon's *Miscellaneous Works* (Vol. V). "Autobiografie (1823)", *Dílo,* I, 31.

[10] The Palacký collection in the *LAPNP* includes in manuscript four catalogues of Palacký's personal library (sign. 11 D 16) and four of Palacký's own long compilations of book titles and authors, reading notes, and excerpts. The latter are entitled: "Europa's allgem. Geschichte der neueren Zeit, 1492-1789: Bibliographische Anmerkungen" (written *ca.* 1820-1821) (11 D 16); "Přípis běžných myšlének a některých listů mých od 1816 násl." (11 C 13); "Slavica. Colligebat. Franc. Palacký Posonii ab anno 1819" (11 C 13); and "Literaria ke krásovědě a historii (z časopisů učených)" (11 D 19). The Manuscript Division of the Library of the National Museum in Prague possesses another library catalogue ("Knihovna Palackého", sign. III B 13) and an additional collection of excerpts: "Anmerkungen und Aufsätze üb. verschied. Gegenstände der Geschichte und Politik. Aus verschied. Schriften gezogen v. Fr. Palacký" (written in 1818) (XVII F 49). Both types of compilations contain references to an impressive variety of works on many subjects, by many authors, and in many languages, ancient and modern. However it is impossible to determine, from these records alone, which of the titles he actually read and how deeply they impressed him. The library catalogues were all made after Palacký's death and do not even reveal when Palacký acquired each volume.

[11] *František Palacký,* 40-41.

find all pertinent sources and to employ them in a critical manner. This part of his training was deferred, however, until he came to Prague. Soon after his arrival, he began taking daily instruction from Dobrovský in the auxiliary sciences and the critical study of source materials. He described his "seminar" to his friends: "My daily occupation is to decipher old scripts, to copy diplomas, bulls, and the like, to copy the titles of Bohemian books and to report on their contents and form." [12] "I spend most of my time there in the study of the sources of Bohemian history. Not books ... but old diplomas, state papers, letters, and manuscripts, which till now have not been printed." [13] "The Master" was pleased with the rapid progress of his pupil, and Palacký himself wrote:

I move now over ground which is classic for me, where everything that I see appears to me in the double image of the present and the past, and which makes me feel sometimes pleasant and happy and sometimes, usually, sad but which always attracts my complete attention, my innermost sympathy. The picture of the whole history of this land becomes ever more alive in my imagination; and when I consider all that greatness, what happened and how it happened, and must see too how it has been presented by our historians till now, you will not wonder that I become ever more eager ... to bring these great men ... out of the darkness of night which surrounds them into the light of day. That the monks, the Jesuits, and their pupils, who alone till now have compiled our history, could neither comprehend nor appreciate the spirit of our ancestors, I do not hold against them; but I must strive all the more to banish the host of phantoms which their sectarianism has brought in, and to give the plain truth to the friends of mankind to see.[14]

Dobrovský was not only Palacký's teacher but his friend (though Palacký steadfastly refused to be considered his disciple). Together with Count Franz Sternberg, he helped to launch his pupil on his historical career.[15] In 1824 he had already set him the task of critically editing

[12] Palacký to Jernej Kopitar, June 22, 1823, *Kor. a záp.*, II, 127-128.
[13] Palacký to Anton Virozsil, June 24, 1823, *ibid.*, III, 81.
[14] *Ibid.*
[15] Palacký was fond of referring to himself as self-taught (*Autodidakt*) in history (*Gedenk.*, 250; *ZBG*, 176). He wrote to Kollár on November 24, 1830: "You are in great error to consider me Dobrovský's protégé and heir; if he were still alive, he would be the first to deny it. He never considered me *his* [disciple], because I had no liking for Slavonic philology ... [and] since 1824 had my own opinions on Bohemian history often opposed to his .... Therefore he was, indeed, often friendly toward me but more often unfriendly, although not always overtly. I always sincerely respected him, ignoring the old man's frailties – for who is free of them? – and I will always honor his memory: but what kinship, what spiritual heritage there existed between him and me, you may decide for yourself." Ant. Jar. Vrt'átko, ed., "Dopisy Františka Palackého k Janu Kollárovi", *ČČM*, LIII (1879), 471-472.

and synthesizing the seventeen anonymous chronicles known as "the Czech annalists of the fifteenth century". In 1825, Sternberg persuaded the Royal Bohemian Society of Sciences to publish them. As has already been related, they appeared in 1829 as the third volume of the series *Scriptores rerum bohemicarum* and constitute Palacký's first important historical work.[16] This was soon followed by the celebrated *Würdigung der alten böhmischen Geschichtschreiber*.[17] A competition for such a work had originally been announced, on Dobrovský's urging, as early as 1804 but without result. In June, 1826, Franz Sternberg had it renewed, no doubt for Palacký's sake, as the latter had been involved in such researches since 1825. Through their combined efforts the prize was awarded to Palacký, but it was the last act of the two benefactors on behalf of their protégé. By the time the work was published in April, 1830, both had died. Nevertheless, their benevolence continued even beyond the grave, for they had already brought Palacký to the threshold of his life's work, to his appointment as Historiographer of the Bohemian Estates.[18]

Palacký further defined his indebtedness to his teacher in his memorial article, "Josef Dobrowský's Leben und Gelehrtes Wirken", *AKBGW* (1833). A Czech translation, "Josefa Dobrovského život a působení vědecké", is available in *Spisy drobné*, III, 418-449; and in *Dílo*, III, 249-282.

[16] Palacký's first historical publications were, of course, the genealogies he composed for the Sternbergs and their friends. Next came his "Spis o zvolení Albrechta Bavorského l. 1440 za českého krále proti nemluvněti Ladislavovi Pohrobku" [On the Election of Albrecht of Bavaria in 1440 as King of Bohemia against the Infant Ladislav Posthumous], which he gave to Count Kaspar Sternberg on October 8, 1826, to be submitted to the censor. Palacký himself wrote: "To počátek (That is the beginning)!" "Každodenníček", *Kor. a záp.*, I, 169.

[17] For details of the writing and judging of the work, see Jaroslav Goll, "Palackého 'Würdigung' ", *Památník 1898*, 247-262. Czech historians are justly proud of the *Würdigung* and fond of pointing out that their rivals, the Germans, did not have anything similar until Wilhelm Wattenbach's *Deutschlands Geschichtsquellen im Mittelalter* (1858). Nevertheless, the work was not completely original: Palacký drew upon such previous studies as Balbín's *Bohemia docta*; Josef Leonhard Knoll's *Mittelpunkten der Geschichtsforschung und Geschichtschreibung in Böhmen und Mähren*; and especially J. G. Meinert's "Aufsätze über die böhmischen Geschichtschreiber des ersten Zeitraums", in Vols. XV-XVI of the *Wiener Jahrbücher für Literatur*. Palacký's negligence in citing his indebtedness to Meinert was caught and severely criticized by an anonymous German reviewer (possibly Knoll) in the supplement to the Leipzig periodical, *Der Komet* (June 18, 1831). The review is reprinted and discussed in J. Pešek, "Nenavistná kritika Palackého *Würdigung*", *ČČH*, XVIIII (1912), 337-340.

[18] Palacký reprinted some of the official documents in connection with his appointment in *ZBG*, 13-48, 83-86. These should be supplemented with others, unavailable to Palacký and pertinent to the proceedings at Vienna, which have been published from the imperial archives by V. Kratochvíl, "Palackého titul stavov-

The last to bear a similar title, though only in general usage and un-officially, had been František Pubička. His *Chronologische Geschichte Böhmens* had begun publication privately in 1770, and when his pub-lisher failed in 1774, Pubička petitioned the Estates to adopt the work, assuring them that it would "immortalize the illustrious deeds of their ancestors and glorify the nation".[19] They agreed in 1777, only to have the venture stopped by imperial decree in 1788 as an unauthorized expenditure and reauthorized in 1793. When publication was stopped again in 1801 (Pubička was eighty years old and ill), the work had reached Volume X (to 1618), with part of Volume XI (to 1630) re-maining in manuscript. Pubička himself died in 1807, and that same year the Estates began their frustrating efforts to have the work con-tinued. They first approached the aged Ignác Cornova, emeritus profes-sor of general history at Prague University. He refused but recommend-ed two of his pupils – František Mikuláš Titze, his successor at the university, and František Němeček, imperial councillor and professor of philosophy. Titze was actually awarded the job in 1808. However, despite constant prodding by the Estates, he wrote almost nothing in ten years and in 1818 asked to be relieved, pleading the pressure of his teaching duties. There followed equally fruitless negotiations with Němeček, Professor Maximilian Millauer of the Prague theological faculty, Baron Freiherr Johann von Stentsch, and others. Each had his own excuse for refusing, but all of them were agreed on the major difficulties involved in writing the history of Bohemia in the seventeenth and eighteenth centuries – the threat of governmental censorship and ill will;[20] the dearth of preparatory studies; and above all the necessity of using vast numbers of primary sources, requiring years of full-time archival research, much of it abroad.

In the autumn of 1827, at Franz Sternberg's suggestion, Freiherr

ského historiografa a státní rada", *ČČH*, XVIII (1912), 321-331 (on the 1830 nego-tiations); and by Josef Pekař, "Palackého titul stavovského historiografa", *ČČH*, XXXII (1926), 376-380 (on the 1838 negotiations). Secondary accounts are J. Emler, "Palacký a české dějepisectví", *Osvěta*, I (1891), 67-75; and Jaroslav Haasz, "K české historiografii", *Památník 1898*, 518-544.

[19] Details of the association between Pubička and his potential successors and the Estates are given in *ZBG*, 5-13; and in Haasz, 518-535.

[20] Pubička's manuscript had ended with the dismissal of Wallenstein from his generalship in 1630. Wrote Palacký, "In the public opinion of Bohemia in the years 1820-1830, the controversy over the guilt or innocence of the Duke of Friedland formed the most delicate and sorest point of all Bohemian history. Everyone feared to compromise himself, either with the public or the government, through a critical investigation of the subject. That was the peculiar reason why everyone chose to refuse the ticklish offer." *ZBG*, 12.

Anton von Bretfeld personally sounded out Palacký for the position. The latter indicated his eagerness to accept it, but pointed out that Pubička's plodding work no longer fulfilled the requirements of contemporary historiography [21] and that its mere completion offered him little personal satisfaction. He asked that the Estates adopt a much broader historical program. But the Executive Committee of the Estates ignored his suggestion and recommended him for the original appointment on October 29, 1827. Palacký responded with a lengthy memorandum on January 24, 1828,[22] emphasizing the need for extensive archival research before any actual writing could begin and presenting a multifaceted historical working program. This included the continuation of Pubička's history to his own day; the writing of a new, complete, and "pragmatic" history of Bohemia in about five volumes; the collection of all existing written resolutions and public proceedings of the Bohemian Estates; the compilation of a *diplomatarium* and *codex epistolaris* of Bohemia; and the writing of special monographs on various related topics. In return, he requested an annual payment of a thousand florins while at work, travel expenses for research trips, funds to hire copyists, and appropriate letters of reference.

In November, 1828, before the Estates had reached a decision another candidate, Josef Edmund Horký, was put forth by Count Mitrovsky and he (Horký) submitted a proposal similar to Palacký's. The two were now requested to sketch their plans in greater detail.[23] Horký's new presentation was a real *tour de force*, rather a detailed exposition of his views on the theory and practice of historiography than a realizable program. On the other hand, he showed his practical inexperience by regarding the problem of source material as a simple matter of accumulating the documents themselves, requiring three years in Bohemia, another in adjoining lands, and several months in Prague to sort his finds. He also requested a permanent post and a regular assistant, a suitable salary and expenses, and funds to purchase horses and a wagon (in which to transport the accumulated documents!). In contrast, Palacký shrewdly presented a somewhat restricted version of his earlier plan which promised to arrive at the desired goal more systematically, quickly, and cheaply than Horký's. These considerations, together with Palacký's

---

[21]   But see Kamil Krofta's more favorable revaluation of Pubička's work: "Frant. Pubička, předchůdce Palackého v zemském dějepisectví českém", *Časopis společnosti přátel starožitností*, LI-LIII (1943/1945), 1-24.
[22]   Reprinted in *ZBG*, 15-20.
[23]   On Palacký *vs.* Horký, see *ZBG*, 25-32; and Haasz, 536-540.

proven reputation and Franz Sternberg's vigorous support, swayed the Estates. On April 13, 1829, they selected him for the post and forwarded his proposed appointment to Vienna for imperial approval.[24]

Here obstacles arose. Neither the honorary award of a similar title to Dobner nor its casual appropriation by Pubička (and even Titze) had created an authoritative precedent for the creation of an official Historiographer of the Bohemian Estates.[25] The contemplated appointment was thus an innovation. Perhaps for this reason the Joint Court Chancellery refused to forward the request to the Emperor, recommending instead that Pubička's work be continued, as before, with a flat rate of payment for each page completed. At the urging of Palacký, who refused to accept such an arrangement, the angry Estates demanded on November 29, 1829, that their proposal be referred directly to the Emperor for his personal decision.[26] Palacký himself went to Vienna in the spring of 1830, where he was personally assured by Counts Saurau and Kolovrat that both the Joint Court Chancellery and the State Council, thoroughly chastened, were now favorably inclined toward the appointment.[27] Nevertheless, after twice setting aside Kolovrat's presentation of the proposal, Francis I finally postponed a decision on it on June 18, 1830, on the grounds that the domestic account of the Bohemian Estates already showed a considerable deficit for 1831. Popular feeling attributed the decision rather to Palacký's Protestant-

---

[24] The cleverness of Palacký's tactics in the competition with Horký becomes more evident in the light of his subsequent career. Once granted the commission, he gradually expanded his efforts to include many of the same auxiliary functions and tasks which had been urged unsuccessfully by his opponent. The total time and expense required by him to complete his assignment also increased greatly. The two men remained in friendly contact for some time; see the four letters from Horký to Palacký, 1828-1840, *LAPNP*, Palacký collection, sign. 11 A 3. In a final postscript to their competition, Palacký reported in 1845 that he and his employers "had purchased in Černý Kostelec an entire archive once collected by Edmund Horký and especially rich in important original documents on the period of the reign of Vladislav III." Palacký to K. J. Erben, September 6, 1845, *LAPNP*, Palacký collection, sign. 11 C 11.

[25] *ZBG*, 4, 12-13.

[26] Wrote Palacký to Kollár, on November 17, 1829: "The Estates of the Bohemian Kingdom at their last meeting elected me their historiographer; the Bohemian Court Chancellery is opposing them in this ... but the Estates wish to have the matter laid before the Emperor himself for his decision. We shall see how it ends." Vrt'átko, *ČČM*, LIII, 394-395. Palacký described the proceedings in much greater detail in a letter to Anton Virozsil, October 23, 1829, ending with the optimistic sentence, "No one here [in Prague] doubts the favorable inclination of His Majesty himself." *LAPNP*, Palacký collection, sign. 11 C 11.

[27] Kratochvíl's documents, which consist of the proceedings of these two bodies and their votes on the issue, confirm this – both supported the proposal.

ism,[28] and there is evidence pointing to the direct, unsympathetic influence of Metternich himself in the affair.[29]

But the Estates were now unanimously determined to do at least what any private individual or group had the right to do – to commission a literary work. Accordingly, on March 28, 1831, they offered Palacký a thousand florins a year, with an additional two hundred florins a year for three years for travel expenses, and commissioned him to write a new history of Bohemia based on original sources, in four or five volumes. The title of official Historiographer was not mentioned, nor any further continuation of Pubička.[30] Palacký accepted, and no overt reaction came from Vienna.[31] His actual appointment as Historiog-

---

[28] Palacký to Kollár, October 1, 1830: "I do not know if I have already written you that the Emperor refused to permit my nomination as Historiographer of the Estates, only, people say, because of my Protestantism, although under another, impersonal pretext . . . . Now our Estates wish to deal with the matter at their next meeting, to decide how they might nevertheless promote me to that office in some other way. The subject has already been under discussion for three years: it is still impossible to see its end." Vrt'átko, ČČM, LIII, 470-471.

[29] Kratochvíl's documents (ČČH, XVIII, 322-323) show that the text of the proposal presented by Count Kolovrat on April 16, 1830, had been corrected stylistically by the Emperor's own hand at that time, i.e., that he was favorably considering its approval and promulgation. On June 18, in Graz, in the absence of Kolovrat but in the presence of Kolovrat's rival, Metternich, the Emperor crossed out the proposal and added a short paragraph rejecting it.

[30] Pubička's work, always a poor seller, met an ignominious end. The remaining copies were donated by the Estates to an establishment for the blind (ostensibly to be read to the inmates), to the troop-education section of Imperial Infantry Regiment Archduke Rainer No. 11, and to the guests' reading-room at the spa in Karlovy Vary. Haasz, 531.

[31] Since Palacký was still to be paid from the Bohemian domestic account, this act of the Estates was a challenge to the imperial decision. The fact that no official action was taken by the Vienna authorities lends weight to the argument that money was not the primary issue. It cannot be claimed that they were unaware of these financial dealings of the Estates. In 1838, when Palacký's appointment was again raised and approved, the Joint Court Chancellery reminded the Estates that their past payments to Palacký had been unauthorized – the Emperor had forbidden such payments and they could not be justified as an expenditure for the continuation of Pubička's history (which *had* been authorized in 1793, but which had been abandoned by the Estates). Now that Palacký had been granted his title, it was suggested that the Estates obtain imperial approval to pay him a regular yearly salary. The Estates, always averse to formalizing any expenditure of their funds, no matter how regular in practice, hedged, and the matter was dropped. Haasz, 542-543. The mild reaction of Vienna to the financial aspect of the matter is in sharp contrast to the immediate investigation which ensued in 1831, when Palacký was rumored to have used the forbidden title in Munich. In June, 1831, when Palacký was working in the Bavarian State Archives, an informer reported that he had represented himself as Historiographer of the Bohemian Estates. An official investigation was initiated and Count Chotek, the Highest Burgrave of Bohemia and President of the Executive Committee of the Estates, was himself reprimanded before it was

rapher of the Bohemian Estates seven years later came as an anti-climax. In 1838 after the death of Francis I, Count Mitrovsky, successor to Saurau as Highest Court Chancellor, suggested to the Estates that a resubmission of their proposal might be favorably received by the new emperor. At Palacký's urging (he confessed to increasing anxiety at his precarious situation as he grew older), they did so in June of that year. They pointed to Palacký's growing reputation, his past industry, and the fact that he had given up all other remunerable employment. They gave assurances that he would not become an official of the Estates with the right to draw a salary, expenses, or pension from any public fund – it was a simple matter of a title. Finally, they reminded the Emperor that a year earlier (April 1, 1837) he had granted similar permission to the Moravian Estates to appoint an official historiographer, Antonín Boček. The coveted title was finally bestowed upon Palacký by Emperor Ferdinand on November 24, 1838.

Palacký set to work almost immediately after he was commissioned in the spring of 1831, following the plan he had outlined in 1828. There followed almost fifty years of broad and systematic historical activity which both preceded and accompanied the writing of the *History*.[32] The task before him was staggering:

Palacký himself had to . . . collect, scrutinize, and publish a mass of material, to bring the Czech past out of the dust and vaults of libraries, to carry out studies of the sources of Bohemian history, to write monographs on the constitutional, religious, literary, and cultural history of Bohemia; and only then could he proceed with his own work.[33]

---

dropped. In his own defense, Palacký wrote to Chotek on June 9, 1831, that the charge was untrue, that in requesting admission to the archives he had signed himself "*Designated* Historiographer of the Bohemian Estates". He had done so, on the advice of the archival officials themselves, in order to bolster his application for admission. With the police he had registered simply as "editor". See O. Odložilík, "Ein Brief Palacký's", *Prager Presse*, May 16, 1926, as quoted and summarized by Pekař, *ČČH*, XXXII, 377, 448; and *ZBG*, 48.

[32] Wrote Palacký to Count Czernin in 1829: "One must first be a diligent historical researcher for half a human lifetime, before one may venture to become an historian." Quoted in Chaloupecký, *František Palacký*, 131.

[33] *Ibid*. The detailed progress of Palacký in carrying out this program, including the writing of the *History*, may be traced through several sources. One is the regular reports on his activities which he was required to submit to the Executive Committee of the Estates, of which the most important are printed, excerpted, or summarized in *ZBG*, 49-72, 86-94, 107-139. Similar unpublished items of somewhat lesser consequence (business and bureaucratic correspondence, financial accounts, publishing statistics, etc.), about 138 items in all, are in the documentary collection entitled "Historiographica: Listiny týkající se jmenování a činnosti Frant. Palackého jako zemského historiografa z let 1827-1872" [Historiographica: Documents Con-

His first step was to investigate all pertinent archives for materials. Although some of his predecessors, such as Dobner and Pelcl, had worked with archival materials, Palacký surpassed them all with his patient, systematic approach. Between 1823 and 1868 he personally visited almost all of the repositories of importance for Bohemian history; every year found him abroad for a few weeks or months. His junior colleague, Anton Gindely, himself an indefatigable traveler to archives, wrote admiringly to him, "In writing your history you economized neither with time nor travel and would surely have gone to America if there had been any sources there." [34] Though these trips drained Palacký physically and mentally, he exulted in the knowledge that they were truly voyages of discovery:

I traveled about cities and the countryside, reveling in the dust of archives and libraries yet untouched, carefully collecting every scrap of old Czech writing, precious and worthless, . . . overjoyed when in the ashes of the past I found a spark which promised to illuminate fields covered by the darkness of forgetfulness.[35]

In the words of a recent evaluator, through his archival researches "Palacký expanded the scale of source material to such a degree that, in this respect, this work may be ranked quite justifiably with the work of Ranke." [36] To be sure, such trips robbed him of the time and strength he needed for the actual writing of the *History*, causing even his enthusiasm to wane at times. In 1833 he complained to Antonín Boček: "I in no way enjoy that mechanical collecting of documents, knowing that it wastes time and torments the soul. I engage in it only because of need, seeing that nobody is really inclined to do this work without which, after all, it is impossible for us to have a national history." [37]

---

cerning the Appointment and Activity of Frant. Palacký as Bohemian Historiographer, 1827-1872], *LAPNP*, Palacký collection, sign. 11 D 17. Another source is Palacký's regular oral contributions to the sessions of the Royal Bohemian Society of Sciences, as reported and summarized in its *Sitzungsberichte*; before 1859, these appeared in the *AKBGW* under the title, "Berichte der wissenschaftlichen Sectionen". Palacký's appearances are indexed in Georg Wegner, ed., *Generalregister zu den Schriften der königlichen böhmischen Gesellschaft der Wissenschaften, 1784-1884* (Prague, 1884), 64-67.

[34] Gindely to Palacký, November 26, 1860, quoted in Kamil Krofta, "Palacký a Gindely", *ČČH*, XVIII (1912), 291.

[35] Palacký, Preface (March 2, 1848) to the first edition of the *Dějiny*, in *DNČ*, I¹, liv.

[36] Josef Polišenský, "František Palacký a naše historická věda", *Zprávy Československé historické společnosti*, I (1958), No. 2, 38.

[37] Palacký to Boček, November 3, 1833, in Boh. Navrátil, ed., "Listy Palackého Bočkovi", *ČMM*, XXV (1901), 106.

Yet in 1868, at the very end of his pilgrimages, we find him as industrious and untiring as at the beginning. From Vienna he wrote to his daughter that despite the unbearable heat and a troublesome cough he worked all day, never leaving his hotel (documents were sent to him from the imperial library), making no visits, and not even reading the newspapers.[38]

Palacký had already visited a great many archives even before 1831. In 1823 his own researches had taken him into the public and private repositories of Prague. Beginning the following year, he went further afield into Bohemia and Moravia and then into adjoining countries. For example, in 1824 he visited, among others, the municipal archives of Budějovice and the private archives of the Czernins in Jindřichův Hradec and of the Schwarzenbergs in Třeboň. In 1825 he inspected the Thun castle-archive in Děčín, the Wallenstein castle-archive in Duchcov, the archives of the Unity of Czech Brethren in Herrnhut in Saxony, and the state repositories in Dresden. In 1826 he spent several weeks in the Lobkovic archives in Roudnice [39] and two months in Vienna, where he often returned and later maintained regular copyists. In May, 1827, he accompanied the publisher Kronberger to Leipzig. After 1831, with the financial support of the Estates, he traveled increasingly abroad. For example, in 1831 he went to Munich; in 1833 and 1835 to Breslau and Oleśnica in Silesia; in 1837 to Rome and Dresden; in 1843 to Berlin, Breslau, the south German cities, and Pest;

---

[38] Palacký to Marie, May 26, 1868, *Rodinné listy*, 235-236. Unpublished documentary material in connection with Palacký's archival researches (e.g., requests to the Executive Committee of the Estates for funds and permission to travel, daily record sheets of repositories visited and documents examined, summary reports and financial accountings to the Estates) are in the "Historiographica" collection in the *LAPNP*. A lengthy manuscript containing Palacký's extracts from sources in numerous domestic and foreign repositories, 1823-1865, has recently been discovered in the Municipal Archives of Pilsen. See the description in Miloslav Bělohlávek, "Příspěvky k bibliografii Františka Palackého", *Časopis společnosti přátel starožitností*, LXVIII (1960), 22-25. Palacký often informed the learned public about his travels and finds, somtimes orally before the Royal Bohemian Society of Sciences, at other times in the Czech Museum journal. See, for example, his "Bericht über die historische Reise nach der Schweitz und dem südlichen Deutschland, besonders nach Basel", *AKBGW* (1849); and "O zahraničných pramenech dějin Českých, zvlášť v XV. století", *ČČM* (1863), on his Lusatian discoveries.

[39] On his activities in Roudnice, an archive rich in manuscripts concerning the Hussites and the Czech Brethren, see Václav Chaloupecký, "Palacký v archivu roudnickém", *ČČH*, XVIII (1912), 332-336. Palacký maintained a lifelong connection with this archive, visiting it again in 1829 and 1862 and having its documents sent to him or copied for him there.

in 1846 to various repositories in Hungary, Austria, Germany as far as the Rhine, and Berlin; in 1849 to Frankfurt am Main, Bavaria, and Basel; in 1853 to Paris; in 1856 again to Dresden and Herrnhut; in 1857 to Munich; and in 1858 to Breslau, Leipzig, and Jena.[40]

Of the domestic archives, the most important for Palacký's researches were the Schwarzenberg archives in Třeboň, once the property of the Rosenbergs and the largest noble archive in Bohemia. Their vast and varied holdings on the Hussites and the fifteenth century were sufficiently complete in themselves, said Palacký, for the writing of a history of Bohemia in that century. He worked there no less than nine times between 1824 and 1868 but despaired of exhausting them.[41] His longest and most important research trip abroad was his visit to the Vatican archives in Rome in 1837. It took four months and was itself a great event for the Czech learned world.[42]

Previous to this, the archives of the Vatican had been made available

[40] A more complete listing of the libraries and archives Palacký visited, especially domestic ones, is given in Zdeněk V. Tobolka, *František Palacký jako politik a historik* (Prague, 1898), 63-64. Other investigations were often made for him by his friends and assistants, as in 1849-1850, when F. L. Rieger and V. V. Tomek both made copies of documents located in the National Library in Paris. See *ZBG*, 124; and four letters from Rieger to Palacký, Nov. 11-Dec. 24, 1849, in Jan Heidler, ed., *Příspěvky k listáři Dra. Frant. Lad. Riegra* (2 vols.; Prague, 1924-1926), I, 67-69, 74. Palacký also regularly acknowledged the help of other historians in securing leads to and copies of manuscript sources (e.g., Burckhardt, Droysen, Erdmannsdörffer, Grünhagen, Höfler, and others – a full list is given in Tobolka, 64).

[41] See František Mareš, "O pracech Palackého v archivu Třeboňském", *Památník 1898*, 114-125, in which Palacký's nine visits to Třeboň have been reconstructed in fine detail from his diary and the register of the archive.

[42] Source material is especially heavy on this trip. The best is Palacký's own published account, *Literarische Reise nach Italien im Jahre 1837 zur Aufsuchung von Quellen der böhmischen und mährischen Geschichte (AKBGW*, 1838, and published separately in that year), including abbreviated reprints of some of the more interesting items found. Six official *acta* are in *ZBG*, 72-83; Palacký's diary entries for the period are in *Kor. a záp.*, I, 190-208. Save for official correspondence, Palacký wrote almost exclusively to his wife. Of the thirty-six letters exchanged between them (March 21-June 14), seven (from his wife to Palacký, with postscripts from Šafařík, Jungmann, and Chmelenský) have been reprinted in Czech translation by Libuše Bráfová-Riegrová, "Z korrespondence Fr. Palackého s chotí jeho Terezií", *Kalendář paní a dívek českých*, XXV (1912), 26-37. See also the published letters from Palacký to Šafařík, May 24, 1837: "Psaní Fr. Palackého P. J. Šafaříkovi", *ČČM*, XI (1837), 362-366 (*Spisy drobné*, III, 679-683); and to Chmelenský, October 10, 1837: "Zprávy z Říma, ze Vlach, a z Čech", *ČČM*, XI (1837), 473-479 (*Spisy drobné*, III, 683-691). All of these sources have been utilized by Josef Borovička in his excellent article, "Palackého italská cesta r. 1837", *ČČH*, XXIV (1918), 165-208. See also the latter's "Palacký e Italia", *Revista italiana di Praga*, I (1927), 39-58.

almost exclusively to the defenders of the papacy. Some modern historians, especially German scholars, had been permitted to use individual sources, but to only one, G. H. Pertz in 1823, had the archives been opened in their entirety. Palacký was the second to enjoy this privilege. His negotiations with Rome began in 1834, carried on in his behalf by Count Kaspar Sternberg, president of the Bohemian Museum, and Count Rudolf Lützow, the imperial envoy to the papal court. The original plan was to have documents copied there. The following year, Count Marino Marini, prefect of the Vatican archives, sent Palacký a catalogue from which he was to make his selections.[43] When this proved too brief and incomplete, the Estates, the Bohemian Museum, and the Royal Bohemian Society of Sciences contributed funds to have a better one compiled. A year passed without result. Meanwhile, in 1836 the first volume of Palacký's *Geschichte von Böhmen* (to 1197) was published, and he felt it imperative to consult papal documents on the thirteenth century, for which the accounts of the Bohemian and Moravian chroniclers were inadequate. He therefore applied to Rome for permission to come in person, receiving it on March 10, 1837. He left Prague ten days later, stopping briefly in Vienna to secure credentials and a visa, and arriving in Rome on April 4.

"I suspect it was a good thing", wrote Palacký, "that I had no idea in Prague of the enormous difficulties which render every such undertaking in Rome impossible; no doubt I should certainly not have set out on this trip." [44] The situation had changed since the friendly reception accorded Pertz in 1823, largely due to the "perfidious behavior" of several subsequent historians, including Ranke, who had used the results of their research in a manner unfriendly to the papal cause.[45] More pressing was the matter of payment. "The whole thing", wrote Palacký, "finally became purely a question of money." [46] Now tempting Palacký with glimpses of rich manuscript treasures, now threatening to cut off all negotiations, the wily Marini bargained with the exasperated Bohemian. Only on April 11, after Lützow had guaranteed appropriate compensation (funds for the trip had again been supplied by the three Bohemian institutions together with the Moravian Estates), could Palacký's researches actually begin. To be sure, he was not permitted

---

[43] *Index monumentorum regnum Boemiae spectantium*, reprinted in *Literarische Reise*, 78-89.
[44] Palacký to Šafařík, May 24, 1837, *Spisy drobné*, III, 679.
[45] Palacký to Count Chotek, April 15, 1837, *ZBG*, 73.
[46] *Ibid.*, 74.

to enter the archives themselves – this was forbidden on pain of ex-communication to all save the Pope, certain papal officials, and, with papal approval, crowned heads. However, like Pertz, Palacký was per-mitted to use materials brought to him in Marini's own home, and the latter assured him that only they two had ever been granted such a concession by the Holy See.[47]

The problem now was one of time. Since the Vatican institutions were closed from mid-June to November every year, Palacký had only ten weeks to complete his research. With remarkable discipline, he worked every day from eight in the morning to six at night, concen-trating on the forty-six volumes of documentary registers of the papal chancellery from Honorius III (1216-1227) to Clement V (1305-1314). By June 16, when he abandoned the archives, he had accomplished a major feat of research: he had systematically examined more than fifty thousand documents and had personally copied or excerpted about four hundred of them.[48] All of the copies were cleared by Marini and the censor, then sealed and sent back to Austria by Lützow through the imperial diplomatic mails. Palacký also examined the Vatican Library for Bohemica, and enroute home he conducted a similar, generally dis-appointing search of the libraries of Florence (the Marucelliana, Riccar-diana, Laurentiana, and Magliabecchiana), the Ambrosian Library in Milan, and St. Mark's Library and the State Archive of the Republic in Venice. He returned to Bohemia on July 24, 1837.[49]

---

[47] Ibid., 76; Palacký to Šafařík, May 24, 1837, Spisy drobné, III, 680.

[48] Palacký to Chmelenský, October 10, 1837, Spisy drobné, III, 684. More pre-cisely, he copied 429 documents, 346 of which were completely new and 246 copied in their entirety. See the annotated chronological list in Literarische Reise, 16-53.

[49] The next of Palacký's countrymen to use the Vatican archives, ostensibly to continue Palacký's researches, was the Moravian Historiographer, Beda Dudík, in 1852-53. After 1880, when the archives were officially opened to researchers, the exodus of Bohemian historians to Rome was led by the enthusiastic traveler, Anton Gindely, in 1882. See Zdeněk Kristen, "Sto let českého výzkumu historického v Římě, jeho dosavadní výsledky a další možnosti", in Za odkazem Františka Pa-lackého (Prague, 1948), 9-51, which traces Czech research in Rome from Palacký to about 1947. Palacký himself made four more trips to Italy in 1838-39, 1844-45, 1847-48, and 1859-60, of which two have also been described by Borovička: "František Palacký – Italská cesta r. 1844", Lumír, LIII (1926), 225-229; and "Palacký v Italii r. 1847", in Vol. II of Od pravěku k dnešku: Sborník prací z dějin československých k šedesátým narozeninám Josefa Pekaře (2 vols.; Prague, 1930), II, 389-395. Though these were not primarily for research purposes (Palacký took his chronically ailing wife to Nice), some information on source materials is con-tained in Palacký's reports: "Zprávy z Neapole", ČČM (1839); and "Bericht über die Nachlese an Quellen für die böhmische Geschichte in Rom", AKBGW (1840).

Palacký thus introduced the majority of relevant archives – domestic and foreign, public and private, secular and religious – to Bohemian historiography. The importance he assigned to archival research had an additional beneficial effect, in that it encouraged the better maintenance and administration of those in Bohemia and Moravia. He himself manifested considerable skill in archival theory and practice.[50] In general, he was opposed to any a priori scheme of archival organization, maintaining that "each archive must be arranged by a sensible archivist in its own fashion and according to the nature of its holdings".[51] He urged archivists to study the contents of their repositories and to study Bohemian history in order to appreciate their significance. On the basis of these principles, he himself made detailed recommendations for the reorganization of the Lobkovic archives in Roudnice in 1826 and, with the help of his assistant, Václav Vladivoj Tomek, prepared a detailed, cross-referenced index, both chronological and topical, to the Thun castle-archive in Děčín in 1840.[52] He also acted as adviser to the Estates on matters concerning the state archives. When he arrived in Prague, he found these in a pitiable condition. For example, the so-called "St. Wenceslas Archive" (*Svatováclavský archiv*), the old archive of the Kingdom of Bohemia and later of the Bohemian Estates, had six locks, the keys to which were distributed among the highest officials of the realm. On the rare occasions when it was opened, a military guard was posted at the door. In 1838, after its contents had been damaged by rain water, Palacký inspected it and recommended its transfer from the chapel of St. Wenceslas to the Prague castle, where he and another of his assistants, Karel Jaromír Erben, restored and catalogued the documents. In 1841-1842 he vigorously opposed a contemplated exchange of holdings between the Royal Prussian Government (the *Kön. preuss. geh. Archiv* in Breslau) and the Bohemian Estates by means of which Bohemian constitutional documents would have been traded for papers of private Silesian families.[53] He did his best to have new archival

---

[50] See Josef Borovička, "Palacký a naše archivy", *Časopis archivní školy*, II (1924), 1-9.
[51] Quoted in Chaloupecký, *ČČH*, XVIII, 335.
[52] Václav Vladivoj Tomek, *Paměti z mého života* (2 vols.; Prague, 1904), I, 160-161.
[53] In his communication to the Estates about the proposal, Palacký reminded them that a century earlier they had resisted the transfer of such documents to Maria Theresa's *Haus-, Hof- und Staatsarchiv* in Vienna and sent copies instead. Moreover, the contemplated exchange of documents with Prussia was hardly a fair exchange – did the Prussians think that the Bohemians could not accurately evaluate such things? Palacký to the Executive Committee of the Bohemian Es-

openings filled by competent candidates. He placed Erben first in charge of the archive of the Bohemian Museum in 1846, then of the Prague municipal archive in 1851 (where after 1864 he was first assisted and then, at his death, replaced by another of Palacký's helpers, Josef Emler). Finally in July, 1862, he successfully urged the establishment of the new, official Archive of the Kingdom of Bohemia (*Zemský archiv*). Designed to be at once an archive and a center for historical research, it was this institution, rather than any individual, which assumed Palacký's position as Historiographer of the Bohemian Estates after his death.[54]

"It is as repugnant to an historian's conscience to demand unqualified, blind belief from his readers", wrote Palacký to his employers, "as it is to refer them to documents with which they cannot be acquainted."[55] Already in 1828 he had pointed to the value of a published collection of the source materials for Bohemian history which would not only serve as a bibliographical supplement to his own *History* and provide the possibility for informed criticism but which would also be of benefit to future researchers. He especially wanted complete and diplomatically-accurate copies of all official documents and letters to 1310, and of the most important ones thereafter to 1347. His plea was repeated and received the sanction of the Estates in 1831.[56] Thereafter his collection of copies grew steadily, especially after additional funds subscribed by the Bohemian Museum in 1841 and a group of eight noblemen in 1843 enabled him to hire several regular helpers.[57] By

---

tates, February 28, 1842, *LAPNP*, Palacký collection ("Historiographica"), sign. 11 D 17 (draft).

[54] See Josef Borovička, "Královský český zemský archiv (1862-1912)", *Zprávy zemského archivu království českého*, IV (1915), 1-143.

[55] *ZBG*, 137; similarly, on the reading public's need and growing desire to check the conclusions of authors against the sources themselves, on p. 88, and in his *Die Geschichte des Hussitenthums und Prof. Constantin Höfler* (Prague, 1868), 6-7.

[56] *ZBG*, 49-50, 54-55, 57.

[57] The noblemen, including some of the greatest names of the kingdom, contributed six hundred florins annually. From 1844 on, Palacký and his helpers (Tomek and Erben) met with these gentlemen annually, exhibiting the year's yield of documents and reading interesting excerpts aloud, after which one of the patrons would invite the whole company to dinner. *Ibid.*, 92-93; and Tomek, *Paměti*, I, 203-204. In May, 1846, the Estates decided to assume the nobles' subvention in the form of payment to an official assistant to their historiographer. For the position Palacký recommended Tomek or Erben, and imperial approval was secured in October, 1846. Meanwhile, the Estates had had cause to change their minds. Their attempt to abolish certain Bohemian offices which they considered superfluous had been denied by Vienna on the grounds that these were "systematized". Fearing a similar fate for any new offices, the Estates (May, 1847) restricted themselves to

1844 his documents numbered more than three thousand.[58] Palacký worked diligently at the project until 1852 when, as a result of his split with the Museum and his preoccupation with the actual writing of his *History*, he was forced to abandon it.[59]

Nevertheless, he was determined to publish at least a selection from his hoard of copies and excerpts.[60] The result was the origin of several collections on Bohemian history which are still of basic value today. Between 1840 and 1872, he managed to publish six volumes of the *Archiv český*, still the most extensive and varied collection of Czech historical documents on Bohemia and Moravia to 1526.[61] His other collections are linguistically mixed and deal exclusively with the Hussite period and the fifteenth century.[62] In Vienna in 1860 appeared his

granting Palacký an additional 600 florins per year, to permit him to continue to hire his own assistants on an *ad hoc* basis. *ZBG*, 109-121; Tomek, "Styky mé s Palackým do roku 1862", *Památník 1898*, 70-72.

58 *ZBG*, 49-92, *passim*.

59 Excerpts from his collection were published by K. J. Erben and Jos. Emler, *Regesta diplomatica nec non epistolaria Bohemiae et Moraviae* (4 vols., covering 600-1346; Prague, 1855-1892). Palacký was also discouraged by the failure of his plan to exchange documents with the Moravian Historiographer, Boček, who was simultaneously engaged on a Moravian *diplomatarium* (*Codex diplomaticus et epistolaris Moraviae*, 5 vols., covering 396-1306; Olomouc and Brno, 1836-1850). Boček's hostility to the idea stemmed largely from the fact that many of his own "finds" were his personal forgeries. See *ZBG*, 60; and the letters of the two men in Navrátil, *ČMM*, XXV, 97-132.

60 He had already published some fragments in the Museum journals. They are listed and partially reprinted in *Spisy drobné*, III, 526-590. Palacký's editorial principles are given piecemeal in his correspondence with Boček (Navrátil, ed., *ČMM*, XXV, 110-111), the *Geschichte des Hussitenthums* (pp. 6-7), and elsewhere. (See also Tobolka, 56; and Chaloupecký, *František Palacký*, 144-145.) Though he criticized Höfler for omitting the learned apparatus in his source publications, Palacký's own collections are weak in the introductions and notes which would assist the reader in comprehending and evaluating the documents printed. He remained primarily interested in determining the genuineness of his finds and transcribing them accurately.

61 Pertinent correspondence between Palacký and the Estates, who published the series, is in *ZBG*, 87-89, 131-132, 137-139. Since Palacký also intended the work to serve as a model of correct Czech diction, only materials originally written in that language were included. See Kristen, "Sto let 'Archivu Českého'", in *Za odkazem Františka Palackého*, 53-71.

62 He also contributed three of his source discoveries on the Council of Basel to the first volume of the series *Acta Conciliorum*, published by the Imperial Academy of Sciences in Vienna: *Monumenta Conciliorum Generalium seculi decimi quinti, Concilium Basileense, Scriptorum*, Tomus I (Vienna, 1857). He himself suggested the series: see his "Bericht an die akademische Commission zur Herausgabe der *Acta Conciliorum*, über die in der Pariser Bibliothek vorhandenen Handschriften zur Geschichte des Basler Concils", *Sitzungsberichte der k. Akademie der Wissenschaften*, Phil.-hist. Classe, XI (July, 1853), 277 ff.

*Urkundliche Beiträge zur Geschichte Böhmens und seiner Nachbar-
länder im Zeitalter Georgs von Podiebrad (1450-1471) (Fontes rerum
Austriacarum*, Abt. II, *Diplomata et acta*, Vol. XX); in 1869 his classic
*Documenta Mag. Joannis Hus vitam, doctrinam, causam in Constan-
tiensi concilio actam et controversias de religione in Bohemia annis
1403-1418 motas illustrantia* (reprinted 1966); and in 1872-1873 the
Urkundliche Beiträge zur Geschichte des Hussitenkrieges (1419-1436)
(2 vols., reprinted 1966). Finally in 1868, when Palacký received a
"national gift" of more than 15,000 florins, the result of a popular
collection organized by the *Svatobor* society for his seventieth birthday,
he transformed part of it into an endowment for the publication of the
ancient narrative sources of Bohemian history to the sixteenth century.
The *Fontes rerum Bohemicarum* began publication in 1873 under the
editorship of Erben and Emler, presenting critical editions of the chronicles of Cosmas, Dalimil, Pulkava, Bartoš Písař, and other domestic
writers as well as excerpts from foreign authors who wrote on Bohemian
history.[63]

In interpreting and evaluating his documents, Palacký was forced
into the auxiliary sciences, then in an entirely undeveloped state in
Bohemia. Already his previous involvement with genealogical research
had shown him the need for a complete genealogical dictionary for
Bohemia and Moravia; of this plan, however, only some separate monographs resulted.[64] Topographical aids were equally lacking. As early as
1834 Palacký had recognized that etymological analysis of place-names
could yield important historical evidence ("Rozbor etymologický míst-
ních jmen československých", *ČČM*, 1834; *Rad.*, I, 128-144; *Spisy
drobné*, II, 248-260). But when he began work on the Hussite period,

---

[63] (8 vols.; Prague, 1873-1932). See Kristen, "Sedmdesát let 'Pramenů dějin českých' ", in *Za odkazem Františka Palackého*, 73-96.
[64] "Einiges über die ältesten Familiennamen des böhmischen Adels" (*Monatschrift
des vaterländischen Museums*, 1829); "Popis staročeských a křestných jmen" [A
Description of Old Czech Personal and Christian Names] *ČČM*, 1832; *Rad.*, I,
115-128; *Spisy drobné*, III, 740-750); "Popis 452 jmen šlechty české i moravské
r. 1415" [The Names of 452 Bohemian and Moravian Nobles in 1415] (*ČČM*,
1834); "Pře rodopisná v Čechách r. 1546 vedená" [A Genealogical Dispute in
Bohemian and Moravian Genealogy and Topography], 453-498. Palacký also
alogy of the Sometime Lords of Zimburg] (Rieger's *Slovník naučný*, II, 1861, 122-
124; *Rad.*, II, 414-423; *Spisy drobné*, II, 324-331); and the appendixes to the *Dějiny*
(1854): "Rodopis Přemyslovcův" [Genealogy of the Premyslids], *DNČ*, I², 342-346;
and "Počátky rodopisu i místopisu českého i moravského" [The Beginnings of
Bohemian and Moravian Genealogy and Topography], 453-498. Palacký also
favored genealogical research as a means of maintaining aristocratic interest in and
support for his historical program.

he saw that the Hussite Wars and the Thirty Years' War had so altered the population [65] and places of Bohemia that a systematic historico-topographical dictionary was absolutely necessary.[66] With the help of Tomek he began to compile one to the end of the sixteenth century, but like its genealogical counterpart, this ambitious scheme was never realized. Of the fragments which were published, the most important was the *Popis království Českého* [A Description of the Kingdom of Bohemia] (Prague, 1848).[67] This was basically a detailed listing in Czech and German of regions, desmesnes, estates, cities, towns, and villages, together with brief statistics (the number of houses and inhabitants) taken from the census of 1843, to which Palacký added thousands of castles, strongholds, and abandoned settlements of which the names had been forgotten or Germanized. It is of special value because it portrays Bohemia under the old feudal administrative divisions which were abolished after 1848.[68]

To help solve the problem of dating documents, Palacký prepared various practical chronological aids. His "Staročeský všeobecný kalendář" [An Old Czech General Calendar] (*ČČM*, 1829; *Spisy drobné*, II, 18-37) was designed to explain the frequent documentary references to medieval holidays. In another work, he carefully identified and dated about two thousand frequently-mentioned personalities: *Přehled sou-*

---

[65] Studies of Bohemian population, past and present, also claimed Palacký's attention: "Gradation der Bevölkerung Böhmens seit den letzten 60 Jahren" (*Monatschrift*, 1829); "Statistisch-topographische Notizen über die Bevölkerung Böhmens im J. 1830" (*Jahrbücher des böhmischen Museums*, 1831); "Historické zprávy o lidnatosti země české" [An Historical Account of the Population of Bohemia] (*ČČM*, 1834; reprinted in *Rad.*, II, 118-130; *Spisy drobné*, III, 185-196).

[66] *ZBG*, 112-116; Tobolka, 65-66.

[67] Other sample entries (Aberspach to Benešov) prepared between 1845 and 1851 were published in 1872 under the title "Zlomky staročeského místopisu" [Fragments of Old Bohemian Topography] in *Radhost*, II, 374-413 (*Spisy drobné*, II, 295-324). Other topographical studies: "Pomůcky k topografii kraje Budějovického" [Aids to the Topography of the Budějovice Region] (*ČČM*, 1835); "Nesnáze starého místopisu a Kostelcové v Čechách" [Difficulties of Old Topography and Places Named "Kostelec" in Bohemia] (*ČČM*, 1851; *Rad.*, II, 357-373; *Spisy drobné*, II, 284-295); and "Ohlídka ve staročeském místopisu, zvláště krajův již poněmčených" [An Examination into Old Bohemian Topography, Especially That of Regions Already Germanized] (*ČČM*, 1846; *Rad.*, I, 144-175; *Spisy drobné*, II, 260-283).

[68] Similar in nature is the map begun by Palacký in 1847 but not published until the year of his death, completed and provided with an explanatory text by his pupil, Josef Kalousek: *Historická mappa Čech, rozdělených na archidiakonáty a dekanáty XIV. století, v nižto jsou poznamenány fary XIV. věku, hrady, mnohé tvrze a j. v.* (Prague, 1876). On Palacký's contribution to geography, see Dušan Trávníček, "Podíl Františka Palackého na vývoji soudobého zeměpisu", *Zeměpis ve škole*, I (1954), No. 4, 121-123.

časný nejvyšších důstojníků a úředníků zemských i dvorských ve království českém od nejstarších časů až do nynějška [A Contemporary Survey of the Highest Officers and Officials of the Land and Court of the Bohemian Kingdom from the Earliest Times to the Present] (Prague, 1832).[69] In his skill in diplomatics, a field then in its infancy, he was the equal of the best of his contemporaries and a worthy pupil of the master, Dobrovský. His theories were laid out and his technique demonstrated in his "Kritická úvaha a výklad základních listin kollegiatního chrámu Litoměřického: Pomůcka k diplomatice české" [A Critical Consideration and Commentary on the Founding Documents of the Collegiate Church of Litoměřice: An Aid to Czech Diplomatics] (*ČČM*, 1836; *Rad.*, II, 188-211; *Spisy drobné*, II, 123-141).[70] Perhaps his greatest personal contribution to this science was his introduction of medieval formularies as an important historical source. These style manuals, containing imperfect copies of various types of documents and letters, had been compiled by chancelleries to guide personnel charged with the framing of similar documents. In time, after the originals of the documents as well as the chancellery registers had been lost, the only surviving copies remained in the formularies. In his acclaimed *Über Formelbücher, zunächst in Bezug auf böhmische Geschichte* (Prague, 2 vols., 1842-1847), Palacký printed over four hundred unknown documents of the thirteenth to fifteenth centuries from Bohemia and neighboring lands which he had found in various formularies, and demonstrated how careful study could extract valuable historical information from them.[71]

---

[69] It is reprinted in *Dílo*, I, 321-417, completed and revised by Jaroslav Charvát. Other works on chronology by Palacký: "O pranostikách a kalendářích českých, zvláště v XVI. století" [On Bohemian Forecasts and Calendars, Especially in the Sixteenth Century] (*ČČM*, 1829; *Rad.*, I, 82-144; *Spisy drobné*, III, 695-719; *Dílo*, IV, 9-34); and the appendixes to the *Dějiny*, I² (1854): "Přehled vyššího duchovenstva v Čechách i na Moravě až do polovice XIII. století" [A Survey of the Higher Clergy in Bohemia and Moravia to the Middle of the Thirteenth Century], *DNČ*, I², 347-370; "Rozdíly krajův a úřednictvo jejich v Čechách a na Moravě" [Regional Divisions and Their Officials in Bohemia and Moravia], 371-439; and "Úředníci dvoru královského až do polovice XIII. století" [Officials of the Royal Court to the Middle of the Thirteenth Century], 440-452.

[70] See also the *Literarische Reise*, 12-15, in which he carefully explains the numerous abbreviations and formulae employed in the documentary registers of the papal chancellery. Unfortunately, so inadequate was the knowledge of diplomatics in his day, that Palacký was often inclined to give equal or greater weight to the content of a document in evaluating its genuineness. This practice at times led him to accept forgeries, such as the "Manuscripts" (see below, Chapter V) and Boček's forgeries.

[71] Originally published in *AKBGW* (1842 and 1847), 5th Series, Vols. II and V.

Even after he had collected his sources, evaluated them, and published them, Palacký still had to extract his data [72] and synthesize them into preparatory monographs before his *History* could progress. He wrote scores of studies of every variety – literary, military, biographical, social, cultural, economic, religious, political, and legal. Most of them originally appeared in the *Transactions* of the Royal Bohemian Society of Sciences or the various journals of the Bohemian Museum, often in Palacký's favorite form, "eine kritische Zusammenstellung und Würdigung aller darüber vorhandenen Quellennachrichten".[73] Surprisingly, even though he was primarily interested in the Hussite period, Palacký wrote little on religious subjects. He was not interested in theological differences and dogmatic quarrels over articles of faith, but in the expression of the national will in Hussitism and in its moral aspects. Hus himself he regarded as a moral preacher rather than a reformer of dogma, and the entire Hussite realm of ideas he left to his successors to study. Only two of his works on religious topics are worth mentioning: the *Předchůdcové husitství v Čechách* [The Precursors of Hussitism in Bohemia], in which he first introduced excerpts from the

---

The work is discussed in Ferdinand Tadra, "Formuláře středověké, důležitý pramen historický" [Medieval Formularies, An Important Historical Source], *Památník 1898*, 263-268. With one last auxiliary science, numismatics, Palacký's experience was slight. See his "Erklärung einiger böhmischen Münzen" (*Jahrbücher des böhmischen Museums*, 1830); and Jaroslav Pošvář, "František Palacký a numismatika", *Numismatické listy Numismatické společnosti Československé*, XII (1957), 83-85.

[72] A glimpse into Palacký's note-system is given in his report to the Estates on March 12, 1836 (*ZBG*, 70-71), in which he indicates that he had adopted about 1835 the device, now an axiom of historical research, of "one note per card": "To deal with the constantly increasing mass of data, which no memory could absorb any longer, I decided henceforth to write every note on a separate slip of paper and to file these slips both alphabetically and chronologically according to their contents and certain headings. I planned special series 1) for historical facts, 2) for archaeological, 3) for genealogical, 4) and for topographical notes, 5) for offices and ranks, and 6) for mixed documents."

[73] A selection of illustrative titles: "On the Modern History of the Bohemian Language and Literature" (1862); "On the Military Art of the Czechs in the Fifteenth Century" (1828); "The Wars of Charlemagne with the Slavs, Especially the Czechs" (1835); "On J. A. Comenius and His Work" (1829); "The History of the Youth of Albrecht von Wallenstein, Duke of Friedland, Sketched for the First Time According to Genuine Sources" (1831); "Bohemian Manners and Morals under the Emperor Charles IV" (1838); "On the Teaching Method and the Oldest Literature of the Taborites" (1850); "Sketch of a General Cultural History of Bohemia" (1831); "The Oldest Epoch of the Fine Arts in Bohemia" (1836); "Précis of a History of Prague" (1836). Palacký also wrote sparingly on non-Bohemian topics – topics in general Slavonic, Hungarian, and Polish history, ethnography, the Indo-European migrations, etc.

thought of such fourteenth-century reformers as Konrad Waldhauser, Milíč of Kroměříž, Matěj of Janov, Jan of Štěkna, and others;[74] and his "O stycích a poměru sekty Valdenské k někdejším sektám v Čechách" [On the Contacts and Relations between the Waldensian Sect and the Ancient Sects of Bohemia], in which he traced the dogmatic influences of the Waldensians on the Czech Brethren and of the Taborites on the Waldensians.[75] On the other hand, because "one can recognize the spirit of the past most strikingly in legal institutions", Palacký was greatly interested in the legal and constitutional history of the Czechs and Slavs.[76] Throughout his studies, like many of his Romantic contemporaries, he was prone to strain the slender evidence and to idealize their ancient politico-economic institutions. Drawing upon Herder as well as a long line of Polish authorities on Slavonic law, especially Joachim Lelewel and his own good friend, W. A. Maciejowski, he insisted that they had originally enjoyed democracy and legal equality and that slavery and serfdom had been foreign to them. In 1830, in his "Zur Geschichte der Unterthänigkeit und Leibeigenschaft in Böhmen", he deduced that serfdom had been fastened upon Bohemia after the Hussite wars by an ascendant nobility under the weak king, Władysław Jagiełło (1471-1516).[77] Because legal sources for the early period were scarce, he ingeniously utilized others. He had frequent recourse to the medieval land registers of Bohemia (*desky zemské*), pointing out that since the thirteenth century many of the decisions of the diets and their verdicts as the highest court of the land had been

[74] The work was written in 1842 and read before the Royal Bohemian Society of Sciences but refused publication by the censor. With Palacký's permission, it was translated into German and published in Leipzig in 1846 under the name of his friend, the well-known Sorbian scholar, J. P. Jordan, and the title *Die Vorläufer des Hussitenthums in Böhmen*. (The agreement is recorded in Jordan to Palacký, June 6, 1846, *LAPNP*, Palacký collection, sign. 11 A 4.) In 1869, a new German edition appeared in Prague under Palacký's own name. A Czech version is available in *Rad.*, II, 297-356; *Spisy drobné*, II, 203-247; and *Dílo*, III, 61-114.

[75] *ČČM* (1868); reprinted in *Rad.*, II, 436-470; *Spisy drobné*, II, 340-364; and *Dílo*, III, 115-144; also in German, *Über die Beziehungen und das Verhältniss der Waldenser zu den ehemaligen Secten in Böhmen* (Prague, 1869).

[76] Palacký, quoted in Pekař, *František Palacký*, 44. See the perceptive evaluations of Palacký as legal historian by Hermenegild Jireček, "Palackého práce o dějinách právních", *Památník 1898*, 485-498; and Theodor Zigel, "Palacký jakožto historik slovanského práva", *Památník 1898*, 499-517.

[77] The article, destined for the *Jahrbücher des böhmischen Museums*, was rejected by the imperial censor "so that such welcome materials could not be misused by the secret scribblers about the countryside to inspire complaints (already numerous enough) by the Bohemian serfs against their masters". *Gedenk.*, 94. The work was first printed in 1874 in the *Gedenkblätter*, 93-103.

copied into these records.[78] When even these failed him, he resorted to Maciejowski's comparative method, collating the laws of the old Czechs and Serbs, for example, to arrive at those of the primeval common Slavonic period: "Právo staroslovanské, aneb Srovnání zákonů cara srbského Stefana Dušana s nejstaršími řády zemskými v Čechách" (*ČČM*, 1837).[79]

In commenting upon this vast and exhausting historical program, Chaloupecký wrote:

Palacký would be a great historian even if he had not written the *History*. What he could not carry out himself he assigned to others. Palacký founded the Czech historical school, created a working program for Czech historiography which only the present generation is slowly accomplishing and which will remain the program of historical work even for future generations. . . .

---

[78] Most of them had been destroyed by fire in 1541, and Palacký urged that they be reconstructed from excerpts and references in other sources. See his "O historické důležitosti starých desk zemských r. 1541 pohořelých a o potřebí i spůsobu obnoviti je, pokud možná, zase" [On the Historical Importance of the Old Land Registers Burned in 1541 and the Need and Manner of Restoring Them Again, as Far as Possible] (*ČČM*, 1863; *Rad.*, II, 424-435; *Spisy drobné*, II, 331-339; *Dílo*, III, 173-184). This was partially acomplished by Emler, in his *Reliquiae tabularum terrae regni Bohemiae a. MDXLI igne consumptarum* (2 vols.; Prague, 1870-1872).

[79] Reprinted in *Rad.*, II, 212-258; *Spisy drobné*, II, 141-176; and as an appendix to the *Dějiny, DNČ*, I² (1854), 295-341. Palacký's source publications and studies in Bohemian legal history were extensive. In 1836, he published part of Viktorin Kornel ze Všehrd's famous early sixteenth-century treatise on the laws and judicial procedures of the kingdom: "Viktorina Kornelia ze Všehrd o právích země České kniha čtvrtá" (*ČČM*, 1836). In 1863, he published the first legal code compiled in Bohemia: *Jura et constitutiones regni Bohemiae regnante Wladislao a. 1500 a M. Roderico Dubravo de Dubrava latinitate donatae* (also in *Archiv český*, V). He also published several private commentaries on Bohemian law of the fourteenth century in the *Archiv český*: "Kniha starého pána z Rožmberka" (Vol. I); "Ordo judicii terrae" (II); "Výklad na právo země české pana Ondřeje z Dubé" (II); and the "Majestas Carolina" (III). He was the disoverer of the famous *Dialogus* of Jan z Rabštejna, written in 1469 by an expert on canon law at the royal court, and published a classic Czech translation of it as an appendix to the *Dějiny, DNČ*, IV² (1860), 583-614. The latter has been reprinted, in shortened form, together with the complete Latin text by Bohumil Ryba in 1942 and again in 1946. Legal studies by Palacký: "Einiges über Geschworenengerichte in Böhmen im XIII. Jahrhund." (*Jahrbücher*, 1831); "Pomůcka k poznání řádů zemských království českého v druhé polovici XIII. století" [An Aid to Understanding the Regulations of the Kingdom of Bohemia in the Second Half of the Thirteenth Century] (*ČČM*, 1831; *Rad.*, II, 177-198; *Spisy drobné*, II, 56-69); "Pomůcky k poznání staročeského práva i řádu soudního" [Aids to Understanding Old Czech Law and Trial Regulations] (*ČČM*, 1835; *Rad.*, II, 146-174; *Spisy drobné*, II, 90-111); "Zur Geschichte der Criminalgerichtbarkeit in Böhmen" (1844, first printed in 1874 in *Gedenk.*, 127-128); and "Příspěvky ku glossarium řeči české" [Contributions to a Glossary of the Czech Language] (*ČČM*, 1827), a small dictionary of archaic words and phrases, mostly legal.

In our historical literature there is perhaps no serious work that is not connected . . . with the historical program of Palacký.[80]

Yet all of this effort had only broken the ground for the *History of the Czech Nation*. Wrote Palacký himself in 1848: "All of my historical writings till now, with the exception of none, I always considered and still consider as preliminary studies, so to say, or simply as preparations for the present work. I think of the *Dějiny národu českého* as the chief and ultimate end of all my endeavor." [81]

[80] *František Palacký*, 131, 150.
[81] Preface (March 8, 1848) to the 1st ed. of the *Dějiny*, in *DNČ*, I¹, lii.

IV

THE *DĚJINY NÁRODU ČESKÉHO*

> Since my youth I have had no dearer or higher worldly aspiration than to present my beloved nation with a faithful picture of its past in which, as in a mirror, ... it might recognize itself and realize what it is and what it should be.
>
> Palacký, *Dějiny*, I¹, Preface (March 8, 1848), in *DNČ*, I¹, li, lviii.

The Estates were impatient with their historiographer, and some members even suspected him of bad faith. In 1831, when they had commissioned him to write a history of Bohemia, they had requested that he state how long it would take him to complete the work. Reminding them of the many years which others, such as Dobner, Pelcl, and Pubička, had found necessary, he had refused.[1] To be sure, he had actually begun writing the first volume in the fall of the following year; and in January, 1833, he reported that he had already completed over half of the first book, on the Boii and Marcomanni.[2] Nevertheless, years passed, and nothing appeared in print. To the Estates' repeated inquiries he replied with patient descriptions of his preparatory researches [3] and once with the weary reminder that "explanations which one has sought and not found and opinions which one has tested and discarded can often be summarized in a few words, although they have cost the researcher a great deal of time".[4]

Publication of the first volume (to the accession of Přemysl Otakar I in 1197) finally took place in November, 1836, late by two months for the coronation of the Emperor Ferdinand as King of Bohemia for which it had been planned.[5] To the despair of the Czech-speaking public, who

---

[1] *ZBG*, 45-46.
[2] *Ibid.*, 61.
[3] E.g., his report of March 3, 1835, *ibid.*, 68-70.
[4] *Ibid.*, 71.
[5] It was based heavily on Dobner. Palacký's sources are cited in his copious footnotes and in periodic topical discussions in the text – there is no separate bibliography appended to the *History*. Instead, he prepared a long bibliographical essay

had eagerly awaited it, it appeared in German – *Die Geschichte von Böhmen, grösstentheils nach Urkunden und Handschriften*. Palacký's agreement with the Estates had presupposed this,[6] and he himself had conceded that it was the only way to reach a wide readership in Bohemia and abroad.[7] Indeed, the work awakened lively interest and praise in both places: two thousand copies were sold the first year, and no less a personage than the King of Saxony expressed his satisfaction with it.[8] The first part of Volume II (to the extinction of the Přemyslids in 1306) appeared in 1839. Thereafter, at three-year intervals followed the second part of Volume II (to the death of Charles IV in 1378)[9] and the first part of Volume III (to the outbreak of the Hussite Wars in 1419).

Palacký's original intention had been to prepare a new and superior Czech version of his *History* only after he had completed it in German. However, when he saw how slowly the work was progressing, he realized that he would have to alter his plan and publish both versions simultaneously.[10] Accordingly, during his vacations in Rome in 1838-

---

on the "Sources of Bohemian History", from the earliest times to his own day, as part of the Introduction to the *Dějiny* (*DNČ*, I¹, 19-37). It requires no detailed discussion. For the pre-Christian period he drew upon the casual references to the Slavs in Roman, Byzantine, and other writers which are still regularly used by modern historians. Beginning with the tenth century, he utilized legends, the chronicles of his predecessors (of which the major ones have been discussed in Chapter I), and a constantly increasing number of original, specialized documents of every variety.

[6]   *Dějiny*, II¹, Preface (March 24, 1875), in *DNČ*, II¹, v.

[7]   In 1873, in the Epilogue to *Radhost* (III, 263), he wrote in retrospect: "In those days, whoever wished to work for the benefit of the Czech nationality had to employ German for the purpose." And in the Preface to the Czech version of his *History* in 1848 (*DNČ*, I¹, lii) he pleaded with his readers not to think that because he had originally written it in German he had preferred to do so.

[8]   To show his appreciation, the king sent Palacký a diamond ring worth about one hundred *Reichsthaler*. The imperial customs authorities promptly levied a duty of sixty per cent upon it, which Palacký claimed he was unable to pay. It took the combined efforts of officials in Dresden, Vienna, and Prague three months to have the impost waived. See Karel Köpl, "Palacký und die Censur", *Památník 1898*, 665-666, n. 38.

[9]   In early 1842, voices were again raised among the Estates requesting more rapid progress and charging that Palacký was deliberately delaying in order to prolong his period of employment. In his "Apologetisches Schreiben" to Count Chotek on February 24, 1842 (*ZBG*, 89-91), Palacký denied this, rejecting the suggestion "that out of the 100 works already published on Bohemian history he was expected simply to construct a 101st", and maintaining that he would never give "either his pen or his name to such a mere compilation". He also demonstrated that it would cost the Estates more if they paid him per volume (as some of the members suggested) than on an annual basis.

[10]   *ZBG*, 128.

Title page of the manuscript of the *Dějiny národu českého* (courtesy of the Manuscript Division of the Library of the National Museum, Prague)

1839 and in Nice in 1844-1845, he began to rewrite the first volume in Czech.[11] Early in 1847 it was sent to the printer,[12] and appeared in the Prague bookstores in March, 1848. It reached the year 1125; otherwise, it was largely a translation by Erben of its German counterpart, with the addition of Palacký's famous introduction on the philosophy of Czech history and an idealized revision of the section on the Czechs in the pagan period. The title of the new version was significantly different, however, and remarkably in tune with contemporary political events in the empire. What had been the *History of Bohemia* was now the *Dějiny národu českého v Čechách a v Moravě* – the *History of the Czech Nation in Bohemia and Moravia*.

As Palacký had planned it, the two editions were to continue companionably side by side, the Czech version subsidized by the *Matice česká* and a private publisher (Calve) and the German one by the Estates, each designed for a different segment of the Bohemian public. But the events of 1848-1849 brought about a fundamental change in his personal outlook. On November 12, 1850, he wrote to the Estates:

My well-known letter to Frankfurt provoked the whole German world against me. For several months the combined German press did not tire of pursuing me with derision and insult, and to this day I am an object of hatred for those who profess German convictions. Because of this offensive situation and since the subsequent acceptance of the principle of the equality of nationalities [within the empire], I have resolved to leave the ranks of German historians forever and henceforth can only compose my work in the Czech language.[13]

---

[11] *DNČ*, I¹, li, lvii. In requesting permission from the Estates to go to Italy in 1838, Palacký informed them that one of his projects while there would be a Czech translation of the *Geschichte von Böhmen*, to satisfy "a wish repeated to me from so many quarters". Palacký to the Executive Committee of the Bohemian Estates, October 1, 1838, *LAPNP*, Palacký collection ("Historiographica") (draft).

[12] "Každodenníček", *Kor. a záp.*, I, 233.

[13] *ZBG*, 123; similarly in the preface (dated October 27, 1850) to the next published installment of the *Dějiny*, covering the period 1403-1424 (Prague, 1850), v-ix, in which he states that since 1848 he has found it "morally impossible" to give precedence to the German readership. In 1849, the *Augsburger Allgemeine Zeitung* wrote that "the entire German nation knows no more hateful name than ... Palacký". (Quoted in *ZBG*, 163.) Yet before 1848 Palacký apparently enjoyed a good reputation as a "German historian", at least in the German learned world. See, for example, the printed invitation sent to him by Pertz personally (and in the name of a distinguished group of scholars including E. M. Arndt, Dahlmann, J. and W. Grimm, and Ranke), requesting his attendance at a scholarly conference of "Germanists" to be held in September, 1846, in Frankfurt am Main. Invited were "men who devote themselves to the cultivation of German law, German history and language". *LAPNP*, Palacký collection, sign. 11 B 6.

To satisfy German readers, a German translation was to be made of the Czech original and published at the same time.

There followed a long and bitter exchange between Palacký and his employers, the Estates, over his decision.[14] On December 30, 1850, the Executive Committee requested "that he let his *History* continue in its previous form". Palacký innocently inquired what this might mean (January 24, 1851). On March 12, the Committee replied that since he had "selected" German for the earlier volumes and this had been accepted by the Estates, they would have to insist that the work continue "as a German original". Palacký rejoined on April 1, claiming that the use of the German language had not been a formal stipulation in connection with his activity and assuring the Committee that he would personally supervise the German translation so that it would not decline in quality.[15] At last on November 6, "in deference to their Historiographer's scholarly reputation", the Estates capitulated, though not without a parting shot – Palacký was forced to cancel his preface to the second part of the third volume of the *Geschichte* which contained a reference to his withdrawal from the ranks of German historians.[16]

Palacký's decision to continue the *History* as a Czech original, though ultimately accepted by the Estates, permanently injured his relationship with his noble employers, who had already been alienated by his political program in 1848-1849.[17] Despite his assurances, it is clear that

[14] *ZBG*, 125-130. The controversy was even reported by an anonymous informer in Prague to the Minister of the Interior, Alexander Bach, in 1850. The former stated that Palacký's pay was to be stopped and that a lawsuit would probably result. Quoted in Friedrich Prinz, "František Palacký als Historiograph der böhmischen Stände", *Probleme der böhmischen Geschichte* (Munich, 1964), 93.

[15] In this respect, he kept his word. He wrote to Johann Droysen on July 13, 1857: "You ask which [of the two versions] is the original. Of course I initially write the text in Czech. After that, however, I polish and rewrite Schulrat Wenzig's German translation to such an extent that this too may be considered an original, since it is not a completely accurate translation in places where the German sense requires and receives more freedom than a translator is permitted to give it." Rudolf Hübner, ed., *Johann Gustav Droysen Briefwechsel* (Berlin and Leipzig, 1929), II, 461. Many translators took a hand at composing the German version, however – not only Wenzig, but Palacký himself, the wife of Anton Gindely, and an unidentified "N. N.".

[16] *ZBG*, 130.

[17] In an interesting study, Friedrich Prinz develops the idea that Palacký had already begun to disassociate himself intellectually from the Estates in the early 1840's and that 1848 simply marks the final parting. Not having really succeeded in his purpose of winning over the Bohemian aristocracy, with its territorial patriotism, to the rising cultural nationalism of the Czech bourgeoisie, Palacký overtly moved his support from the former to the latter. In 1848, in his book as in his politics, he stopped being the scholarly mouthpiece of the interests of the Bohemian

from that time on he really lost complete interest in the *Geschichte von Böhmen*, lavishing his attention upon the *Dějiny*. To be sure, some of the earlier sections of the Czech version were simply translations from the previously published German version. Many, however, were different from and superior to their German counterparts, having been written on the basis of more than ten additional years of knowledge and experience gained through the writing of the *Geschichte*.[18] On the other hand, the first three German volumes themselves were never revised; not even their censored sections were restored to correspond with the corresponding uncensored sections of the *Dějiny*. As for the Estates, they were never happy with the change and apparently expressed their dissatisfaction by deliberately delaying their approval to publish the installments of the *Geschichte* – at least Palacký could not be persuaded that their behavior was anything but intentional and based purely on their antipathy to him.[19] Their ill will culminated in 1859-1860, when the Executive Committee took from January, 1859, to March, 1860, to approve the publication of Volume IV, Part II (covering the reign of George of Poděbrady, 1457-1471).[20] Then on April 10, 1860, because the Czech version had already appeared earlier, the Committee warned Palacký, on pain of terminating its financial support, that in the future the German edition was to appear not later but rather earlier than the Czech one, and thus to preserve the impression that it was the original.[21] The threat of losing his employment was a constant one after 1848-1849, and Palacký was always conscious of it.[22] For example, he

---

Estates. "František Palacký als Historiograph der böhmischen Stände", in *Probleme der böhmischen Geschichte* (Munich, 1964), 84-94.

[18] Palacký certainly did not hide the fact that he considered the German volumes already written simply part of his preparation for the *Dějiny*. See *DNČ*, I¹ (1876), lii. In 1863, when giving permission to the Pole, J. Chociszewski, to translate the *History* into Polish, he urged him to use the Czech version as a base: "The Czech text is different in many ways from the German; it is worked up much more thoroughly and correctly." Palacký to Chociszewski, December 25, 1863, *LAPNP*, Palacký collection, sign. 11 C 11 (copy).

[19] In 1853, the situation seemed so unpromising that F. L. Rieger urged Palacký to find his own publisher for the German edition. Rieger to Terezie Palacká, March 28, 1853, in Heidler, *Příspěvky*, I, 173.

[20] There is much discussion of this particular delay in Palacký's correspondence: e.g., Palacký to A. V. Šembera, March 26, 1859, and December 8, 1860, *LAPNP*, Palacký collection, sign. 11 C 11; Palacký to Tomek, series of letters from November 23, 1859, to April 25, 1860, sign. 11 C 11 (copies); Rieger to Palacký, January 25, 1860, and April 7, 1860, in Heidler, *Příspěvky*, I, 123-125.

[21] *ZBG*, 136-137.

[22] Tomek records that already in 1849 there was doubt that the post of historiographer would be continued under the new political conditions, with the old diet

wrote to his son Jan on January 9, 1860, warning him not to be extravagant or to expect financial aid from home: "I do not know what awaits me in the nearest future. It appears that the Executive Committee of the Estates is just lying in wait for the opportunity to be able to deprive me of my present payment. Certainly it [the Committee] burns with hatred against me as against our whole nationality; and while injustice reigns in the state, it is impossible to depend upon anything." [23] Palacký's sole significant defense against this threat seemed to him to be to stir up the greatest possible publicity and demand for his work among German readers. On July 18, 1857, he wrote to his publisher, Friedrich Tempsky, urging him to send copies of the *Geschichte* liberally to the German press and journals and to hire someone to keep track of the resulting reviews of it: "Publicity is my shield, and I am in need of protection." [24]

To take advantage of the suspension of censorship in 1848 and to avoid interrupting the progress of his research, Palacký postponed writing the remainder of Volume I and all of Volume II in Czech and began Volume III, on the Hussite period. It appeared in two parts in 1850 (1403-1424) and 1851 (1424-1439). Volume III of the German edition was advanced to the same terminal date, in two additional parts, in 1851 and 1854. In the latter year, Palacký also completed Volume I of the Czech edition (to the beginning of the reign of Přemysl Otakar II in 1253). This was followed by Volume IV ("The Age of George of Poděbrady") – Part I (1439-1457) in 1857, Part II (to George's death in 1471) in 1860; and Volume V ("The Age of the Jagellonians") – Part I (1471-1500) in 1865, and Part II (to the Battle of Mohács in 1526, when the Bohemian crown passed to the Habsburgs) in 1867. The German edition was now complete, but Volume II of the Czech edition was still lacking. But Palacký, provoked by the criticism of Constantin Höfler (see below) and to incorporate the wealth of new material he had acquired on the Hussites, first completely revised Volume III (in three parts, 1870-1872) before filling the remaining gap – Part I (1253-1333) in 1875, Part II (1333-1403) in 1876.

---

dissolved and the character of the future one unclear. *Paměti*, I, 325.
[23] Palacký to Jan, January 9, 1860, in Zíbrt, *Osvěta*, XXXIX, 154-155.
[24] Palacký to Tempsky, July 18, 1857, *LAPNP*, Palacký collection, sign. 11 C 11. Jan Palacký reported that Tempsky remained his father's chief supporter in 1859, assuring the historian that if he were dismissed by the Estates he would "take him into better-paid service". "Intimní vzpomínky na Fr. Palackého", *Památník 1898*, 128.

He died about a month after the last section appeared in print.[25]
A suitable motto for the *Dějiny národu českého*, wrote Goll, might
be "pro populo bohemico".[26] It pictured the Czech nation as

small, indeed, but richly gifted, unusually progressive, enlightened, devoted
to productive and useful work; not aggressive but heroic, fighting gloriously
not only for its own life and its own independence and freedom but for
the highest treasures of human society; greatly responsible for the progress
of humanity, but suffering cruelly through the disfavor of fate, the malice
of its neighbors, and the lack of inner concord.[27]

Such a portrayal could not help but inspire Czech readers, but others
had cause to feel differently. Dealing with a period when the Czechs
were still their own political masters and centered about the "heretical"
Hussite Revolution,[28] it immediately awakened the secular and religious
watchdogs of the empire. The Bohemian Germans also had a grievance.
By design, the *Dějiny* concentrated upon "the history of the Czech nation in Bohemia and Moravia" and devoted much less attention to the
German inhabitants of these areas.[29] Still worse, Palacký characterized

[25] A new Czech edition, the so-called "3rd edition", embodying all of Palacký's
revisions, was seen through the press after his death by his assistant, Josef Kalousek
(5 vols. in 11; Prague, 1876-1878). It is the one most frequently consulted by
scholars. Reprintings of individual parts of both versions are given in Zíbrt, *Bibliografie české historie*, II (1902), 796-797; and a complete listing of the fifteen editions of the *Dějiny* published between 1848 and 1941 is given in Milan Machovec,
Fr. Palacký a česká filosofie (Prague, 1961), 101, n. 159. Palacký himself prepared
a précis of the *History* for Rieger's *Slovník naučný*, II (1861), 375-388: "Stručný
přehled dějin Českých doby starší (až po r. 1526)" [A Brief Survey of Bohemian
History in the Old Period, to 1526] (reprinted in *Rad.*, II, 487-538; *Spisy drobné*,
II, 376-413). The work also provided a major part of the material for Francis
Lützow's well-known *Bohemia: An Historical Sketch* (1st ed., London, 1896; rev.
ed., 1939).
[26] *ČČH*, IV, 270.
[27] Vásclav Vlček, "Dějepisecké dílo Františka Palackého", *Osvěta*, VI (1876), 402.
See the similar, but much longer and more rhetorical summary of the nature of
the history of the Czech nation by Palacký himself, *DNČ*, I¹, 13-15.
[28] One of Palacký's critics, Constantin Höfler, labelled the *Dějiny* (quite correctly)
as a history of the Hussites, with a long introduction on the older period and an
unwritten epilogue on the period after 1526.
[29] Or to regional Moravian history. This defect especially pained Palacký, himself of Moravian birth. He attributed it chiefly to the reluctance of the Moravian
Historiographer to share his collection of source-materials with him. Palacký's
critical reference in his Preface of 1848 to "men who believe that Moravian patriotism should be anti-Czech" is probably an allusion to Boček. *DNČ*, I¹, lviii. See
also J. Pošvář, "Z listů F. Palackého A. Bočkovi o poměru Čechů a Moravanů"
[From the Letters of F. Palacký to A. Boček on the Relationship of Czechs and
Moravians], in *Rodné zemi* (Brno, 1958), 140-145; also Chapter III, n. 59. Palacký's
genuine interest in Moravian history and historiography is evident in his extensive
correspondence with various learned Moravians. See, for example, A. Neumann, ed.,

the Germans as originally a nation of predators (*Räubervölker*), whose aggressive competition with the peaceful Slavs formed the kernel of Bohemian history. Criticism thus descended upon the work from all sides, beginning with the publication of the first volume in 1836, mounting sharply after 1848, and continuing until well after Palacký's death – indeed, to the present day.

Like all authors of the empire before 1848, Palacký was compelled to submit his writings to the judgment of the imperial censors in Prague and Vienna and, in order to avoid complete prohibition, to delete passages and insert interpolations at their request.[30] As editor of the Museum journals he had frequent altercations with them, and works of his own which were refused publication have already been mentioned. Until the mid-1830's, his *bête noire* was Father Jan Václav Zimmermann, a priest and Knight of the Cross and chief of the imperial censorship in Prague. As early as 1824 Palacký wrote to Kollár in Pest of the "haughtiness and extreme foolishness" of the censor, "who behaves like an autocrat, knowing that as a state official the police will take his part against all complaints";[31] and in 1831 he wrote to the poet, Karl Egon Ebert, that "the tyranny of Pope Zimmermann's censorship has finally become unbearable to me".[32] Yet Palacký's relations with the censors were not always so strained. Sometimes the latter would return an article to him before making a formal decision, requesting further explanation or suggesting changes which would make it acceptable.[33]

Acta et epistolae eruditorum monasterii ordinis S. Augustini Vetero-Brunae (Brno, 1930), *passim*; and Milada Wurmová, ed., "Neznámé dopisy Františka Palackého: Příspěvek k historiografii", *ČMM*, LXXIII (1954), 322-339.

[30]   See the good synthetic treatment by Karel Köpl, "Palacký und die Censur", *Památník 1898*, 646-688; and brief supplementary documentation by Jos. Volf, "Palackého dějiny a censura", *ČČM*, LXXXVII (1913), 157-158. Köpl has combined part of Palacký's own account with the correspondence between the executive officials of Bohemia (the Bohemian *Landespraesidium*), censorship headquarters in Vienna (the *Polizei- und Zensurhofstelle*), and its branch in Prague (the *k. k. Bücherrevisionsamt*). Drawing upon Palacký's manuscripts, he even reprints passages which were altered or expunged as they originally appeared. Since the censored sections of the *Geschichte von Böhmen* were never reprinted as Palacký had originally written them, Köpl's article is an indispensable supplement for those using the German edition. See pp. 684-687, n. 63.

[31]   Palacký to Kollár, January 22, 1824, *Kor. a záp.*, II, 164.

[32]   Quoted in Goll, *ČČH*, IV, 28. In 1835 he also wrote satirically to Boček that Zimmermann had agreed to permit the printing of Ludwig Spohr's oratorio, *Des Heilandes letzte Stunde*, only if the name "Jesus" were everywhere removed. Palacký to Boček, November 24, 1835, in Navrátil, *ČMM*, XXV, 123.

[33]   Palacký's replies in two such cases are reprinted in *Gedenk.*, 103-109; and in *Spisy drobné*, III, 512-515; and should be supplemented with additional primary

On other occasions, as in the case of his *Geschichte von Böhmen*, he was able to draw upon the influence of his supporters among the Bohemian nobility and the highest officials of the kingdom. Largely through the efforts of Count Chotek, the Highest Burgrave of Prague, the first two volumes (1836-1843) were handled with dispatch by the Vienna authorities and escaped with only minor changes.[34] But not even Chotek's successor, the Archduke Stephan, could shield Palacký when the work reached the third volume, on the Hussites. Wrote the latter: "As long as I had to contend only with political censorship, things went well; but now that theologians have been called in to decide on my description of Hussitism, many errors and shortcomings are being discovered." [35] The proceedings are a classic illustration of the enormous difficulties under which scholars had to work in Metternich's Austria.

In November, 1843, Palacký submitted the second installment of Volume II, on the beginnings of Hussitism (1403-1414). It was returned the following March with a long row of alterations and excisions demanded, chiefly on theological grounds – it was considered unfriendly and injurious to Catholicism. Palacký's description of the widespread corruption of the Catholic clergy at the beginning of the fifteenth century was deleted, and Hussitism chiefly attributed to the "stubbornness, inflexible obstinacy, and dogmatism" of Hus himself. Palacký was

---

material in Köpl, 647-656. One of these, in 1834, concerned his critial evaluation of the legend of the martyrdom of St. Wenceslas ("O umučení sv. Václava, podlé legendy slovanské, úvaha kritická"). The censor returned a tentative verdict of *Damnatur*, protesting that Palacký had not depicted Drahomíra, the mother of St. Wenceslas, as a heathen and co-author of her son's death, although this was a centuries-old item of popular religious belief. But Palacký held to his historical judgment, maintaining that "if the verdicts of legends and of general public belief were to be set up as a rule for history, all historical research would come to an end". *Spisy drobné*, III, 513. He also used the familiar argument that the article was not likely to be read by the general public. Nevertheless, it was not permitted to be printed until 1837, when it appeared in the *ČČM* (XI, 406-417) – still in censored form (it was subsequently reprinted in full in *Rad.*, II, 131-145; and *Spisy drobné*, II, 79-90).

[34] Manuscripts were generally returned in about a month or less. Köpl (661, n. 28) has prepared a table showing when sections of the work were submitted and returned. Chotek's offer to save time by doing the censoring personally in Prague was not accepted by Vienna: "Provincial insight in such things was deemed insufficient and inadmissible." Palacký, *ZBG*, 94.

[35] Palacký to Virozsil, December 28, 1844, *LAPNP*, Palacký collection, sign. 11 C 11. Palacký's correspondence with the censors about this volume is reprinted in *ZBG*, 94-107; selections from it have been translated into English by Lützow in his *Historians*, 95-97, and his *Literature*, 396-398.

warned by Count Sedlnitzky, head of the *Polizei- und Zensurhofstelle* in Vienna that "the Austrian government, as the chief protector of the Catholic church, cannot allow that, in a work appearing under its censorship, periods of domestic church history be treated in a spirit hostile to the ruling religion". Referring to "the previously noticeable inclination of the author to Czechism at the expense of the German element", he also warned that "in a state where many nations are united under one scepter and give their allegiance to a ruler of German blood, it cannot be allowed that one nationality attack, disparage, or undermine the others, especially not the ruling one." [36] The next installment (1414-1419), including the description of Hus before the Council of Constance, fared much worse. Palacký submitted it at the end of June, 1844, with the plea that the censoring be expedited so that he could oversee the printing of the manuscript before his departure from Prague with his ailing wife for Nice, scheduled for early October.[37] By September 20 it still had not been returned by the censor, and Palacký, complaining of the delay, requested the Estates to permit him to delegate to Tomek and Erben the task of seeing the installment through the press in his absence.[38] Finally, on September 30, the manuscript returned. The censor, a professor of theology named Scheiner, had allegedly urged that the entire manuscript be suppressed, charging that it was "sometimes an open, sometimes a concealed apology for Hus and his cause" and that the author was acting as "Hus's attorney", swaying the reader in his favor, discrediting his accusers and judges, and seeking to paint him as without faults and a martyr. The case was ultimately referred to Metternich himself, who decided that the author was to be allowed to state facts but was to avoid all "missliebige Raisonnements".[39] Scheiner thereupon demanded a long series of changes to make the work palatable to Catholic readers. For example, in reply to Palacký's statement that even Hus's enemies had admired his courage before the Council, he wrote: "The Catholic church does not discern in [Hus's attitude] unshakeable courage but insolence and obstinacy founded on deep delusion." [40] As for the famous letter from the papal secretary, Poggio Bracciolini, to Leonardo Aretino praising the life and death of

---

[36]   Quoted in Köpl, 669, 670, 671.
[37]   See the draft of Palacký's letter (no addressee), June 30, 1844, *LAPNP*, Palacký collection ("Historiographica").
[38]   Palacký to the Executive Committee of the Estates, September 20, 1844, *LAPNP*, Palacký collection ("Historiographica") (draft).
[39]   *ZBG*, 95-96.
[40]   *Ibid.*, 98.

Hus's colleague, Jerome of Prague (d. 1416), which Palacký had cited, Scheiner doubted both its authenticity and the credibility of its author.

When the mutilated manuscript was returned to Palacký, he was in the midst of last-minute preparations for the journey to Nice. Before he left, however, he penned a detailed and sharply-worded reply. He disclaimed any intention of misleading Catholic readers: "My wife and children and many of my closest friends are ardent Catholics, and it has never occurred to me to wish to offend them or divert them from their faith." [41] In fact, he claimed that he had even solicited opinions about the manuscript from his Catholic friends before submitting it for censorship.[42] As for the Bracciolini letter, he was amazed that Scheiner was not acquainted with it since it had been cited by Aeneas Sylvius (later Pope Pius II) himself in his *Historia Bohemica* and had since been passed by the censors and reprinted many times: "If contemporary Catholic theologians appear so much more anxious about judging their adversaries than Popes and papal secretaries of the fifteenth century, should I not conclude that their anxiety goes much too far?" [43] If he had given Hus more virtues than faults, it was partly because the most detailed sources had been provided by Hus's adherents, partly because of "the undeniable importance and worth of the man":

According to my innermost convictions and, I think I may add, according to the verdict of every *impartial* judge, Hus intended only good, even though the means which he chose were not all free of sin and therefore not completely blameless. In this sense I have tried to write about him with the greatest possible impartiality and believe that my account is quite compatible with a genuinely devout Catholic interpretation. If I have been mistaken in certain details, I will gladly yield to correction. I cannot, however, believe that it is indispensable for Catholicism that every deed and thought of Hus be condemned a priori, that he be painted entirely in black, and that all circumstances which appear to favor him, even if they are completely corroborated historically, should be suppressed. Such a one-sided and unjust presentation would no longer be history but a party-pamphlet. Unfortu-

---

[41] Quoted in Köpl, 677. This sentence is missing in the abbreviated text printed in *ZBG*, 100.
[42] Robert von Zimmermann reported that, in the early 1840's at Palacký's request, a group of scholars and friends met in the home of the philosopher, Bernard Bolzano, and Palacký read to them sensitive passages from his history of the Hussites. "The scrupulous historian, who wished neither to renounce historical truth nor to come under suspicion as a Protestant, to deny his personal confession of faith unfair influence upon his presentation of religious controversies, subjected his description to the verdicts of those whom he knew to be as broad-minded and just in religious as . . . in national things." *Památník 1898*, 43.
[43] *ZBG*, 105.

nately, the censor seems to expect something of that nature from me. Should this apprehension be justified, I regret to have to declare that I cannot and will not ever accede to such a demand. I would rather give up all my work and withdraw my hand from the writing of history. For an historian also has his high and extensive obligations, which must be as sacred to him as are, for instance, those of a professor of dogmatics or an inquisitor.[44]

Having made his defense, he bowed to the inevitable and declared himself willing to make those changes deemed absolutely imperative. He asked only that the final decision not be left to the present censor but "to another, reasonable man, who knows how to combine the necessary Catholic zeal with a little Christian love".[45] Public knowledge of Palacký's wrangling with the censors only increased popular interest in the forthcoming installment of the book, and diverse rumors circulated in Prague about the matter. "Some think that the publication of the *History of Bohemia* has been completely forbidden and stopped forever . . .; others say that because of this you have emigrated from Bohemia and that you will do your writing abroad . . .; and there is more", wrote the amused Tomek to him.[46] But Vienna was not amused. Sedlnitzky, writing in November, 1844, to the Archduke Stephan, protested the unsuitable tone of Palacký's reply and instructed him to inform Palacký officially of the government's displeasure. Stephan passed the instructions to the Executive Committee of the Estates, which refused to administer the rebuke on the grounds that Palacký was not one of its officials. Stephan then referred the matter to the Prague police chief, Muth, who duly reprimanded Palacký when he returned home in May, 1845.[47] This was the last of Palacký's major troubles with the imperial censorship, however. None of the subsequent installments of the *History*, in either language, apparently suffered much from it, and all traces of it were ultimately removed from the earlier volumes of the Czech version.[48]

---

[44]   *Ibid.*, 101-102.
[45]   *Ibid.*, 106. The final changes, which turned out to be rather minor, were made by Tomek and Erben. See Tomek to Palacký, November 26, 1844, January 14, 1845, and March 7, 1845, *LAPNP*, Palacký collection, sign. 11 B 9; also Tomek, *Paměti*, I, 198-199; and his "Styky mé s Palackým", *Památník 1898*, 69.
[46]   Tomek to Palacký, January 14, 1845, *LAPNP*, Palacký collection, sign. 11 B 9.
[47]   Muth to Palacký, May 8, 1845, in *ZBG*, 107.
[48]   Nevertheless, from Palacký's correspondence it is probable that the difficulties the *Geschichte* encountered in 1859-1860 were partially due to censorship, at least in the sense that the Estates delayed approval of the work out of fear of the displeasure of Vienna and of the Prague consistory, which was allegedly considering forbidding faithful Catholics to read it. In 1860, Palacký even feared that the police would confiscate the corresponding section of the *Dějiny*, already in print.

The void left by the censors was rapidly filled by a variety of German adversaries.[49] Palacký's letter to Frankfurt in 1848 had made him the target of the German *Hetzblätter*. To this the *Dějiny národu českého*, appearing almost simultaneously, added the weight of German scholarly criticism ("a criticism characterized by a spirit more German than scholarly", observed Palacký [50]). Every conclusion, every characterization of a person, an incident, or even a source which was unflattering to the Germans was heatedly challenged.[51] Palacký replied patiently to the more important of his critics – to have answered all of them, he wrote, would have required the lifespan of Methuselah.[52] To be sure, one of Palacký's most persistent and under-handed opponents began his activity long before 1848. Josef Leonhard Knoll, at one time (1832-1838) a professor of general and Austrian history at Prague University and ostensibly Palacký's friend (Palacký had recommended him for membership in the Royal Bohemian Society of Sciences in 1834), was a passionate defender of a centralized and Germanized Austrian empire

---

See Palacký to his son Jan, January 9, 1860, January 30, 1860, and February 16, 1860, in Zíbrt, *Osvěta*, XXXIX, 154-156; and Anton Gindely to Palacký, January 12, 1860, and February 10, 1860, *LAPNP*, Palacký collection, sign. 11 A 3.

[49] There were Slav critics, too, most notably Jernej Kopitar, the Slovene philologist who had acted as imperial Slavonic censor in Vienna. Material on his differences with Palacký, more personal than scholarly in nature, is given in *ZBG*, 145-153; and in Köpl, 656-658.

[50] *Dějiny*, II¹, Preface (March 24, 1875), in *DNČ*, II¹, vii. No systematic study of the German reviews of the *History* has been made. Since the work was reviewed as it appeared, in installments, and since the reviews generally are found in literary periodicals to which access today is difficult, such a study is not very feasible. (See the list of selected reviews of the *History* and of several other of Palacký's works in the *Památník 1898*, 722-723). In his brief survey, "Jak byla posouzena německými učenci vědecká činnost Fr. Palackého", *ČMM*, XXII (1898), 331-337, Rud. Dvořák concludes that prior to 1848 German scholars generally evaluated Palacký's work justly and favorably, and that the best of them continued to do so even after 1848 (as evidenced, for example, by the Palacký necrologies presented before the Vienna and Munich academies, of which Palacký was a non-resident member, in 1876, the latter by Wilhelm Giesebrecht). This is certainly corroborated by the published correspondence between Palacký and Droysen. The twenty-one letters exchanged between them between 1856 and 1865 betray nothing but mutual respect and a warm scholarly friendship. There is not a trace of rancor between the Prussian apologist and the Bohemian who viewed Prussia as a dangerous threat to the Slavs. See Rudolf Hübner, ed., *Johann Gustav Droysen Briefwechsel* (2 vols.; Berlin and Leipzig, 1929), II, *passim*.

[51] Thus in 1846 Palacký was forced to defend himself against attacks in the *Augsburger Allgemeine Zeitung* that he had favored Přemysl Otakar II (admittedly one of his favorites) in the account of the latter's struggle with Rudolf of Habsburg. See *ZBG*, 154-160.

[52] *ZBG*, 176.

and ever vigilant for any sign of a cultural or political awakening on the part of the Czechs, whom he considered potential traitors to the House of Habsburg.[53] In a long series of secret communications to the Highest Chancellor, Count Mitrovsky, he first denounced various enterprises with which Palacký was intimately associated – the Czech journal of the Bohemian Museum, the *Matice česká*, and even the acceptance of Czech as one of the official languages of the Royal Bohemian Society of Sciences. In 1836 he attacked the first volume of the *Geschichte von Böhmen* before his students and the next year prepared a covert critique of it for Vienna. He urged that the work be suppressed before it created "thirteen million Slavs burning with national fanaticism and hatred against the Germans".[54]

A more formidable antagonist was Constantin Höfler, Knoll's successor at the university and once Palacký's close friend.[55] Because of Höfler's comprehensive restatement of previous German and Catholic arguments, Palacký labelled him "the chief representative of anti-Hussitism in historical literature". In 1856, Höfler began publication of his *Geschichtschreiber der husitischen Bewegung in Böhmen* (*Fontes rerum Austriacarum*, Series I, Vols. II, VI, VII, Vienna, 1856-1866), in which, by shrewdly selecting and commenting [56] upon the texts of

[53] See the study of Knoll's activities, based on his previously secret correspondence, by František Dvorský, "Frant. Palacký a náš nepřítel", *Památník 1898*, 443-472; also *Gedenk.*, 129-131; and *Spisy drobné*, III, 515-517.
[54] Quoted by Dvorský, 467. There may have been a personal element involved – apparently Knoll had come to Prague with the idea of becoming Palacký's assistant and had been rebuffed. As for Palacký, he wrote to Boček: "Knoll is especially vexed because I do not think of the old Slavs and Czechs as barbarians, brutes, and savages, as he imagined them." Palacký to Boček, December 16, 1836, in Navrátil, *ČMM*, XXV, 126.
[55] According to Tomek (*Paměti*, I, 375), in 1851 Palacký had recommended Höfler for the position at Prague University. One can trace the estrangement between the two men through Palacký's letters to his daughter Marie (in *Rodinné listy*). On November 1, 1852 (p. 70) he described a visit he had had from Höfler and Mrs. Tempsky, the German wife of Palacký's publisher. In a long tirade, Höfler surprisingly maintained that the German nation had grown old and had outlived itself in history. Palacký in turn found himself in the unlikely position of moderating Höfler's remarks in an attempt to reassure Mrs. Tempsky who, "comprehending them only with a woman's feelings, was worried to death, as if the end of the world were at hand". On June 6, 1860 (p. 167) he wrote to his daughter and son-in-law from Geneva, asking them to thank Höfler for proofreading the latest volume of the *Dějiny* in Prague. Finally, on May 26, 1868 (p. 236) he wrote from Vienna: "Höfler is here; we are mutually ignoring one another."
[56] Volume III of this work contained more of Höfler's personal commentary than it did of original texts. In a rare lapse into humor, Palacký observed that "one must assume that Herr Höfler had reserved a place for himself among the *Geschicht-*

the Hussite chroniclers, he placed one-sided stress on the antagonism of the two Bohemian nationalities and thus tried to portray the movement in the most unfavorable light. This view was then repeated in his *Magister Johannes Hus und der Abzug der deutschen Professoren und Studenten aus Prag 1409* (Prague, 1864). Palacký replied with his own documentary publications (see above) and with his classic polemic, *Die Geschichte des Hussitenthums und Prof. Constantin Höfler* (Prague, 1868).[57] "That work of mine created such a sensation here", wrote Palacký elatedly to the French Slavist, Louis Leger, "the first edition was completely bought up in several days in Prague alone, so that booksellers elsewhere have not yet received any copies at all". A second edition was immediately rushed into print to meet the demand.[58] In the first half of this work he cited hundreds (out of thousands, he claimed) of Höfler's serious errors and distortions in publishing Hussite sources, thus effectively destroying his reputation as a paleographer and editor. In the second half he replied to Höfler's view of the Hussite period. Höfler had unconditionally condemned it. Hus himself was "not only a heretic, but also a common criminal". The Hussite Revolution was "a harmful historical phenomenon", "a badly-disguised conflict of nationalities" ("eine deutschenfeindliche nationale Revolution"), with the religious element of only secondary importance.[59] In his rebuttal, Palacký presented a memorable restatement (and perhaps a revision) of his characterization of the Hussites, laying heaviest emphasis on their moral and religious aspirations.[60]

---

schreiber whom he was offering to the public and that he even yielded himself precedence". *Die Geschichte des Hussitenthums*, 15.

[57] Parts of this work have been translated into Czech by F. M. Bartoš, *Obrana husitství* (Prague, 1926); and in *Spisy drobné*, I, 295-299; a few passages are given in English by Lützow, *Historians*, 103-105.

[58] Palacký to Leger, February 20, 1868, *LAPNP*, Palacký collection, sign. 11 C 11.

[59] Höfler, quoted in *Die Geschichte des Hussitenthums*, 68.

[60] Palacký's views on the Hussites, as well as the question of a possible reorientation of his views brought about by the Höfler controversy, are discussed in Chapter V. An interesting repercussion of the Höfler affair is cited in the Palacký entry in Constant von Wurzbach, *Biographisches Lexicon des Kaiserthums Österreich*, XXI (Vienna, 1870), 191-192. In 1858, in celebration of its tercentenary, the University of Jena decorated the residences of its former students who were now famous men with memorial tablets bearing their names. Allegedly one was also erected for Palacký who, to be sure, had never been a student there but who owed much to German schooling and had contributed signally to Austrian historiography. After the Höfler interchange (in which Palacký had again characterized the Germans as insatiable aggressors), various German newspapers, especially *Die Gartenlaube* (Leipzig), for years demanded that it be removed. In November, 1876, in the Palacký obituary which appeared in this periodical by Friedrich Schütz ("Auch ein

The matter did not end there, however. The very next year Höfler himself returned to the attack in a series of articles in the *Mitteilungen des Vereins für Geschichte der Deutschen in Böhmen,* an organization which he had helped to found in 1861 and which henceforth served as a rallying-point for German criticism in Bohemia.[61] As the century progressed and the political, economic, and cultural rivalry between the Czech and German inhabitants of the kingdom sharpened, the debate increasingly abandoned scholarly channels, and all of Palacký's pleas that national, religious, and personal polemics be excluded from historical discussions went unheeded. The Germans held to their dictum that the Czech nation "had been able to divest itself of its inborn bestial nature only as far as it had been led toward humanity by the Germans".[62] Palacký, like Hus himself, was accused of being a German-hater. These charges provoked him into a final, passionate rejoinder:

When, where and how have I so insulted or injured [the German nation] that it has the right to treat me as an enemy? I have never been conscious of an evil intent against the Germans. ... It has never occurred to me to deny or to detract from their great significance in the history of the world; even at this moment I do not feel myself the opponent of the entire nation, but of a few persons who make it their business to disparage and ridicule *my* nation.

I admit that in writing my work ... I have not described Bohemian history according to the traditional German viewpoint. That is to say, I have always held ... that the Czech nation exists through the grace of God, not the grace of other nations, and that it is entitled to preserve and improve its existence without regard for the Germans, and even against their will. Consequently, primarily its weal and woe, and not that of the Germans, has served me as ... the guiding principle by which I have evaluated events. ...

---

slavischer Agitator"), it was stated that this had been done. In 1898, Rud. Dvořák (*ČMM*, XXII, 333) again made official inquiries of the burgomaster of Jena as to the fate of the Palacký tablet. The reply was that no such tablet existed, nor was Palacký's name on the list of such tablets. Dvořák concluded that the Germans had indeed destroyed all traces of it. Nevertheless, as Palacký was never a student at Jena, it is not impossible that no such tablet ever existed.

[61] See *ZBG*, 161-216; and *Die Geschichte des Hussitenthums,* 82-83. Palacký tried to counter the attack of German scholars on Hus by sending his own publications to sympathetic foreign scholars with the plea that they publicize them among their countrymen. To Leger he sent copies of his *Documenta Mag. Joannis Hus,* observing: "I would wish that this book be well advertised in France, England, and America, because in recent times the Germans have increasingly become enemies of Hus, not only for his alleged hatred toward Germans (invented by Höfler) but also because he somewhat dims and diminishes the glory of their Reformation, of which they are so proud." Palacký to Leger, May 24, 1869, *LAPNP*, Palacký collection, sign. 11 C 11 (copy), Leger collection, sign. 20 P 71 (original).

[62] Quoted by Palacký, *ZBG*, 163; and in *Spisy drobné,* I, 324.

The old Czechs fought more than three-fourths of their historic wars in defense against the repeated attacks and encroachments of the Germans. The latter cannot simultaneously claim the glamor and advantage of a conqueror and the praise of a gentle, peaceable nation; one reputation excludes the other. And whoever can believe that the Germans undertook their bloody campaigns against the Slavs only through the altruistic impulse to civilize them, and that they therefore have always been in the right – with him it is impossible to discuss history.[63]

Further altercations with German scholars resulted from Palacký's involvement in the famous literary dispute, the "Battle of the Manuscripts".[64] This revolved not about his *History* but about the authenticity of two sources upon which he had relied heavily – the Queen's Court [*Rukopis královédvorský – RK*] and Green Mountain [*Rukopis zelenohorský – RZ*] manuscripts. The *RK* was "discovered" in 1817 in a church in the Bohemian town of Králové Dvůr by Václav Hanka, a noted Czech philologist of the time. It consisted of twelve sheets of parchment containing lyric-epic poems and songs in archaic Czech, and was accepted as genuine by no less an authority than Dobrovský, who dated it in the late thirteenth century. The *RZ* appeared in 1818, allegedly sent secretly from Zelená Hora by the Czech steward to Count Colloredo-Mansfeld to be part of the collections of the Bohemian Museum. It consisted of four sheets of parchment containing the first hundred and thirty-two lines of the poem "The Verdict of Libussa".

---

[63] *ZBG*, 164, 160; similarly to Leger, March 17, 1876, *LAPNP*, Palacký collection, sign. 11 C 11 (copy), Leger collection, sign. 20 P 71 (original). At least one of Palacký's German friends, the Silesian historian Colmar Grünhagen, defended him against the charge of being a Germanophobe: "It is scarcely conceivable psychologically that one would write nine imposing volumes [the *Geschichte von Böhmen*] in good German, with warmth and animation, who really, seriously hated and despised this nation. It is simply that the interests of the Czechs mean more to him." "Fr. Palacký: Ein deutscher Historiker wider Willen", *Preussische Jahrbücher*, XXVIII (1871), 243.

[64] A brief description in English of the controversy is given by Paul Selver, *Masaryk* (London, 1940), 120-139; and in German by Plaschka, *Von Palacký bis Pekař*, 47-50. In Czech, it has twice been summarized by F. M. Bartoš: *Rukopisy* (Prague, 1936), and *Rukopisy Královédvorský a Zelenohorský* (Prague, 1946). Most of Palacký's contributions to it are reprinted or excerpted in *Gedenk.*, 67-77, 214-259; and *Spisy drobné*, III, 547-590. Palacký also discussed the "Manuscript" controversy extensively in his correspondence with A. V. Šembera, the Moravian archivist. See Palacký to Šembera, March 26, 1859, and April 29, 1859, and Šembera to Palacký, March 24, 1859, April 21, 1859, May 3, 1859, and May 21, 1859, *LAPNP*, Palacký collection, sign. 11 C 11 and 11 B 8. Selections in English from the "Manuscripts" themselves are in Sir John Bowring's *Cheskian Anthology* (London, 1932). The latest edition of both "Manuscripts" is a new translation in modern Czech by Kamil Bednář (Prague, 1961).

Dobrovský branded in a forgery, but other authorities accepted it as genuine and dated it in the ninth or tenth century, thus making it the oldest specimen of Czech literature in existence. Both documents were eagerly seized upon by Czech scholars, artists, and the general public as fuel for the National Revival, for they testified to advanced cultural and civic conditions among the Czechs far earlier than had been imagined. Wrote Hanka:

Just as the Greeks, the Argonauts, the Heroes before Troy and the Seven Greeks on the battle-field of Thebes – just as these found their Homer, Aeschylus and Orpheus; so, too, our ancient poets such as Lumír and Záboj sang of the renowned deeds of bygone Heroes, the wars of princes, the life-and-death contests of the yeomen, the joys and sorrows of love and other suchlike adventurous matters. . . .[65]

Even Goethe admired the poems, and Hanka, as their "discoverer" and "translator", gained considerable fame.

Palacký accepted the genuineness of the "Manuscripts" from the very first and thereafter defended them against all criticism, despite mounting evidence that they were forgeries and sometimes to the point of straining scholarly credulity. In 1829, in the Wiener Jahrbücher für Literatur, he announced his acceptance of the RK ("Über die Königinhofer Handschrift und deren Herausgabe durch Hanka und Swoboda"), "the star of ancient Czech culture and national independence fallen into oblivion", and in 1834 followed suit for the RZ in the Czech journal of the Bohemian Museum ("Časopisové čeští r. 1834" [66]). In 1840 he and Šafařík published a critical edition of the RZ along with other ancient (and likewise disputed) fragments in Die ältesten Denkmäler der böhmischen Sprache.[67] It was a brilliant display of external and internal criticism and added considerable scholarly weight to the "Manuscripts". However, to explain the queer script of the RZ, Palacký was forced to argue the improbable hypothesis of a special old Czech school of paleography. The controversy was revived in October, 1858, when the Prague daily, Tagesbote aus Böhmen, printed a series of anonymous articles under the title "Handschriftliche Lügen und paläographische Wahrheiten", in which Palacký's hypothesis was rejected, the "Manuscripts"

---

[65]   Quoted and translated in Selver, 125.
[66]   ČČM, VIII (1834), 462-465.
[67]   Palacký also supplied the critical annotations to excerpts from the "Manuscripts" which were published in two contemporary anthologies: Výbor z literatury české (2 vols.; Prague, 1845-1868), Vol. I, ed. J. J. Jungmann; and Gedichte aus Böhmens Vorzeit (Prague, 1845), translated and edited by Count Joseph Matthias Thun.

labelled as forgeries dating from about 1817, and Hanka named as the forger. Although Hanka himself was only with difficulty persuaded to sue the editor, Palacký did not hesitate "to defend our holy cause before the learned world". The next month, in a series of articles under the same title in the periodical *Bohemia*, he waged a skillful defense of the beleaguered sources. For one thing, he claimed, the *RK* contained historical data unknown to historians until 1829. For another, the combined talents of "Hanka, myself, 'Anonymous', and several dozen of his partners" would not be sufficient to create a literary work equal to the "Manuscripts".[68] Now foreign scholars entered the fray. In 1859, the Viennese professor, Maximilian Büdinger, published an article in the *Historische Zeitschrift* ("Die Königinhofer Handschrift und ihre Geschwister" [69]), in which he proved that the data in question had already been available to researchers in the eighteenth century. Palacký's reply ("Die altböhmischen Handschriften und ihre Kritik") in the same volume was weak and ended with the hope that "other writers will replace me in this endless, unwelcome dialogue".[70] Goll characterized Palacký uncharitably but accurately: "Palacký was a man of firm convictions and strong will. He did not change much. . . . Whatever he decided, in that he persisted. . . . His favorite word was 'unyielding' [*neoblomný*]. He carried on a discussion or a debate . . . as long as he could expect others to submit, but he stopped when he himself would have to yield and rather took no further part in the matter." [71] Though Palacký later expressed some doubt as to Hanka's complete innocence, he held stubbornly to his views on the "Manuscripts" until his death. To be sure, he regarded the controversy (quite correctly) as far more serious than a mere literary-historical squabble among savants. While vigorously rejecting all suggestions that his own nationalism had blinded him and dictated his judgment, he saw in the German attack a concerted attempt to discredit the Czech nation and its leaders. He wrote to A. V. Šembera that "our dispute over the old manuscripts has greater significance and

[68] Similarly in his detailed reply to the detailed published criticisms of his *Geschichte von Böhmen* made in 1837 by a German author writing under the pseudonym "Cosmas Luden", who charged him with over-reliance on the forged "Verdict of Libussa". Palacký's reply appeared in F. A. Brockhaus's *Repertorium der deutschen Literatur und Allgemeine Bibliographie für Deutschland* (Leipzig), "Bibliographischer Anzeiger", 1838, No. 4, pp. 17-19.

[69] *HZ*, I¹ (1859), 127-152.

[70] *HZ*, I³ (1859), 87-111. To Palacký's anger, the editor of the *HZ* (von Sybel) delayed the publication of this issue until Büdinger could compose a rebuttal ("Entgegnung auf den Aufsatz des Herrn Palacký", 112-117).

[71] *ČČH*, IV, 253-254.

deeper foundations than appear to the eye. I am convinced that the
stimulus to it issued and still issues from Vienna. . . . Our blameless
behavior is extremely repugnant to the designs of that group which is
determined to use every means to undermine and destroy our moral
position and that esteem and regard which we enjoy in the nation. If
this attempt does not succeed, another and still another will follow.
. . ." [72]

As long as Palacký was alive, Czech critics themselves, out of
deference and perhaps out of fear of the old man, moderated their
attacks on the "Manuscripts". However after his death, in the 1880's,
a coalition of Czech scholars – paleographers, philologists, historians,
and even chemists – rapidly discredited them as forgeries, most probably
the work of Hanka and his friends, V. A. Svoboda and Josef Linda.
Prominent in the coalition were Jaroslav Goll and T. G. Masaryk, one
the opponent, the other the defender of Palacký's interpretation of the
national history.

[72]   Palacký to A. V. Šembera, March 26, 1859, *LAPNP*, Palacký collection, sign.
11 C 11.

V

THEORY AND PHILOSOPHY OF HISTORY

> As regards the principles and intentions which have guided
> me while working at this history, I have hardly a word to
> say. I know of no others, except those that proceed natural-
> ly from the supreme principle of regard for historical truth.
> ... I hope ... that my sincere craving for truth, my respect
> for all laws, divine and human, my zeal for order and legal-
> ity, my sympathy with the weal and woe of all mankind
> will preserve me from the sin [of partiality] ....
>> Palacký, *Geschichte von Böhmen*, I¹ (1836), Pref-
>> ace (August 23, 1836), vii.

> Whoever wishes to write the history of our nation must
> carefully consider all the circumstances [which have shaped
> it] ..., must know the characteristics of the national spirit
> perfectly, must understand sublime sentiments and great
> deeds, and must ascend to the concept of the life of nations
> – then will he create an immortal work.
>> Palacký, "Každodenníček", April-July, 1819, *Kor.
>> a záp.*, I, 36.

Like many another important historian, Palacký never prepared a systematic exposition of his theory of historiography or of his philosophy
of history.¹ Consequently, although their chief elements were probably
developed in the 1820's and 1830's, these must be pieced together or
deduced from a great number and wide variety of statements and
sources composed over sixty years – from his scholarly works in various
fields (especially the *History*), his political speeches and articles (especially the epilogues to *Radhost* and *Gedenkblätter*), his polemical

---

¹ He did contemplate such syntheses, however. On March 24, 1820, he recorded
in his diary that he had sketched the beginning of an essay entitled "O dějinách a
dějopisectví" [On History and Historiography]. *Kor. a záp.*, I, 73. This was never
mentioned again. And in 1867 he informed the public of his intention, once the
Dějiny was completed and revised, of writing monographs on the significance of
Bohemian history for European history and on the spirit of Slavonic history in
general and Czech history in particular. *DNČ*, I¹, Preface (March 3, 1867),
viii. Unfortunately, he died before these could be written.

writings and reviews, contributions to newspapers, letters, and diary entries. Such a reconstruction has been attempted by various scholars, usually philosophers rather than historians, most successfully and with greatest care by Josef Fischer.[2] The latter insists that Palacký was a remarkably consistent thinker whose philosophical ideas form a system, not always consciously or clearly formulated or apparent but "latent".[3] Nevertheless, even Fischer's synthesis is not fully convincing. One who has significantly immersed himself in Palacký's writings cannot escape the suspicion that all such elaborate schemes are highly artificial, and that Palacký's philosophy has been made much more complete and coherent than it actually was. What follows deals with its most important elements, even these, unhappily, not without their ambiguity.

Preceding chapters have depicted Palacký the historian at work and have shown that the method he utilized may justly be called "modern". There remains to see what he considered the nature of history and the historian's task to be in theory.[4] It is generally accepted that in this sphere he drew heavily upon four eighteenth-century English authors: two historical theoreticians – Hugh Blair (*Lectures on Rhetoric and Belles Lettres*, especially lectures 35 to 37, on history) and Lord Bolingbroke (*Letters on the Study and Use of History*), and two practicing historians – Edward Gibbon (*Decline and Fall*) and William Robertson, the Royal Historiographer of Scotland (*The History of Scotland during the Reigns of Queen Mary and King James VI till His Accession to the Crown of England*). Palacký characterized history at various times, in terms mundane ("History is the presentation of everything that happened, renewed by speech"), rhetorical ("History is the dearest heritage of a nation"; "To write history is to erect temples to deeds and bridges across forgetfulness"; "A nation deprived of the history of its forbears is like an unfortunate foundling who yearns and inquires in vain for his parents and family"), and highly idealistic:

---

[2] *Myšlenka a dílo Františka Palackého* (2 vols.; Prague, 1926-1927), esp. I, 17-206, and II, 9-198; abridged in his *František Palacký o minulosti pro budoucnost* (Prague, 1926), esp. 3-47, 90-97. Fischer has read exhaustively in Palacký's works, published and in manuscript, and has excerpted and paraphrased pertinent passages from them. The reader is referred to the notes to Fischer's study for citations to such passages. In this work, only the most important citations are given.

[3] Fischer, *Myšlenka*, I, 8, 11. The same view is apparent in the recent, Marxist-oriented study by Josef Válka, "La théorie de l'histoire chez F. Palacký", *Sborník prací filosofické fakulty Brněnské university*, 1967, No. 14, pp. 79-100. Like Fischer, Válka "recreates" Palacký's theory of history by reordering and synthesizing his scattered statements and interpolating much that seems logically implied in his actual historical writing.

[4] See especially Fischer, *Myšlenka*, I, 103-115.

History in general is the final product of the enlightenment of nations. History, in the higher and correct sense of the word, originates only where a nation, spiritually aroused and united for social ends in a state with its own laws, struggles against its obstacles of its own free will, and where that struggle is so gripping that the memory of it is eagerly renewed. Only where the nobler part of man rules over the sphere of merely animal activity, where human life through its yearning for ideas and deiformity acquires a higher significance and the spirit is not mired in the slime of triviality or exhausted by the poison of sensuality, where the names of God and country, law and virtue, right and freedom awaken such response in the soul that the whole community is ready to defend them even with its own blood: only there can deeds take place which are dear enough and worthy enough to be recalled for posterity. Life without principles is completely beyond remembrance and therefore does not even deserve to be related.[5]

History in general is the final temporal judgment over those who distinguished themselves by their activities on the world-stage, a human judgment, of course, and therefore neither infallible nor sufficiently competent. ... Indeed, in the name of all humanity, every historian performs a function of no less importance in the service of truth and justice than a judge called to defend civil society.[6]

An historian's task is even harder than that of an ordinary judge, continued Palacký, because he must seek all of his testimony among the dead. It is not often that he is fortunate enough to be supplied with evidence sufficiently copious, detailed, many-sided, and trustworthy to facilitate a confident and easy verdict. Nevertheless, he is bound by his sources: "he must not create freely according to his own fancy". Since every important historical event is based on the conflict between two opposite forces (see below), the eternal law of justice requires that the testimony of both sides be heard and considered without pre-judgment. Where a decision is difficult, it must be made with reservations or not at all, lest the historian exchange his role of judge for that of partisan.

Not only in dealing with sources but in all historical activity the primary requirement is honesty – the historian must be as objective and impartial as is humanly possible. Wrote Palacký to Kollár in 1830: "History does not suffer any foreign designs on her field; she demands to be developed and revealed from herself. I am not dedicating myself to her service in order to tear her out of German paws but in order to see her truly, let the chips fall where they may." [7] This view was repeated in his review of Lichnowsky's *Geschichte des Hauses Habsburg*

---

[5] *DNČ*, I¹, 7-8.
[6] *DNČ*, II¹, 199.
[7] Palacký to Kollár, November 24, 1830, in Vrt'átko, *ČČM*, LIII, 472.

in 1837: "She [history] has only one purpose, but an all-encompassing and holy one, and therefore a higher and independent value; she ceases to be our teacher as soon as we make her our servant." [8] That he was sincere is shown by his disparagement of the immoderate claims then being made for the character of early Slavonic history. In refutation of Kollár's theory that the name "Slav" was derived from "sláva" [glory], and in contrast with his own later idealization of the old Slavs, he wrote: "On what was that glory based before the fifth century? The Germans conquered world-ruling Rome; our Slavs could not resist the Huns or the Germans, nor did they conquer the Byzantines." [9] And he warned another friend, Vinařický: "I always and everywhere have sought, am seeking, and shall seek only for the truth. . . . If you take up research in order to discover as much [that is favorable to] Slavdom as possible in antiquity, I fear that not truth but [the cause of] Slavdom will be your aim." [10] Of course he realized that complete objectivity is unattainable: "Only inexperienced theoreticians can demand of an historian that all so-called subjectivity disappear from his work: in reality we know of no great historian whose particular spirit is not reflected in his writing, as in a mirror." [11] Moreover, objectivity does not entail indifference to the perpetration of evil; the historian's task is not merely to report on events or to draw lifelike pictures of the past but to make moral judgments and conclusions.

If the historian is to use sources of every type, and since every variety of human history is his province,[12] it follows that he must possess

[8] *Spisy drobné*, III, 677. And again: "If history is to be our teacher, we must not make her our prostitute." *DNČ*, III[1], 10.
[9] Palacký to Kollár, November 24, 1830, in Vrt'átko, *ČČM*, LIII, 472. Even his beloved Hussitism was to be portrayed with strict impartiality, "to be weighed on the strict scale of enlightened reason and Christian faith", so that each should get "his deserved praise or shame" as truth demanded. Recorded in Palacký's "thoughts" in the manuscript entitled "Běžné myšlenky a opisy. Od r. 1817 a násl. 7. Dějopis Hussitstva", *LAPNP*, Palacký collection, sign. 11 C 13.
[10] Palacký to Vinařický, 1834, quoted in Chaloupecký, *František Palacký*, 153.
[11] Review of Lichnowsky, *Spisy drobné*, III, 677.
[12] See Palacký's Introduction to his *Würdigung*, quoted in Chapter I. In this respect, his own *History* is deficient. In the *Dějiny*, non-political history is treated chiefly in five small sections of Books ii, v, vii, x, and xiv, in which Palacký gives "a picture of public life" in Bohemia in the pagan period and in the thirteenth, fourteenth, and fifteenth centuries. Such data were simply not yet available, and even his own numerous preliminary researches could not adequately supply them. He himself was aware of this shortcoming of his *History* and hoped to correct it by writing a supplementary volume summarizing all of the changes which had occurred between 1253 and 1526 in the organization and administration of the Bohemian state and in the moral, legal, and social conditions of the Czech nation. *DNČ*, V[2],

many talents and wide experience. He especially needs mature philosophical and psychological insight. An historical account must be something more than an indiscriminate recital of critically-ascertained facts. An historian must have the ability to select the most significant incidents and characters, especially those of importance for the spiritual development of mankind, and to elicit their causes and effects, to penetrate to their innermost nature: "An historian is an artist if he is able to describe surely and clearly the external life of his subject as a reflection of its inner life." [13] Other aspects of "historical art", such as an accomplished style, balance in the organization of whole and parts, and a talent for enlivening details, are subordinate though related and not to be disdained. Palacký stated several times his desire and intent to write a "pragmatic" history of Bohemia; and though he did not define the term it seems clear that he was referring to the qualities just mentioned and that he was employing the term in the common eighteenth-century, especially eighteenth-century German sense.[14]

Even if all of these foregoing requirements are met, one may hope only to approximate the truth. Complete historical truth is forever ruled out by the inadequacy of evidence and the mortal limitations of the researcher himself:

I am far removed from the presumption of believing that I have always found the truth. The historian who can believe that has certainly never understood the seriousness of research. God alone sees into the heart . . .: man, however, judges everywhere from appearances, . . . which often deceive us in the case of contemporaries, even friends. How could we hope to derive nothing but truth from the . . . deficient transmissions from the past? Honest investigation and effort are all that can be demanded and given.[15]

Preface (March 3, 1867), vii-viii; *Geschichte des Hussitenthums*, 1; and A. V. Šembera to Palacký, May 21, 1869, *LAPNP*, Palacký collection, sign. 11 B 8. This, too, was prevented by his death.

[13] Quoted in Pekař, *František Palacký*, 43-44.

[14] Compare, for example, the definition by J. L. von Mosheim: "A pragmatic history is a flowing and therefore lively description of certain connected events, where the events are explained, as far as is possible, from their causes, and where the major figures are portrayed according to their nature, abilities, and customs. Everything should be ordered and presented so that the non-scholarly reader as well as the scholar will not only be entertained but also taught to know himself, his world, and true common sense." *Versuch einer unpartheiischen und gründlichen Ketzergeschichte* (Helmstedt, 1746), 28. I am indebted to my former colleague at the University of California at Los Angeles, Professor Peter Reill, for bringing this definition to my attention.

[15] *Geschichte von Böhmen*, I¹ (1836), Preface (August 23, 1836), vii.

Moreover, our conception of the truth may change with the passage of time:

From one side, the diligence of researchers brings to view an increasing number of historical sources hitherto unknown, from the other, human vision acquires a broader and clearer perspective . . . ; and just as recent events may be explained from the past, so past events often gain unsuspected light from the present.[16]

These fundamental principles, rigorous yet realistic, easily satisfy the criteria of "scientific" historiography. But Palacký had not taken up the study of history solely or even primarily for its own sake. Like Boling-broke, whose famous dictum he carefully copied out, he envisioned history "in the higher sense" as a teacher of wisdom to the present – *Historia magistra vitae*. From the very first, he repeatedly stressed that his own work was to be instructive for contemporary generations, that it was to help revive the Czech nation. He agreed with the Englishman that history was to aid in the development of "a general system of ethics and politics on the surest foundations" and that one must apply himself to it "in a philosophical manner and spirit". In short, Palacký's theory of historiography had to come to terms with his philosophy of history, and Palacký the scholar with Palacký the nationalist.[17]

Palacký's general philosophy of history is part of his personal philosophy of life, the latter itself only partially formulated in connection with his (likewise incomplete) philosophy of aesthetics.[18] Of primary

[16] *DNČ*, V², Preface (March 3, 1867), ix.
[17] "Next to [Palacký] the scientific historian there always stands the philosopher, the moral judge, the politician, and the pedagogue (especially the 'awakener')." Fischer, II, 217.
[18] Palacký's writings on aesthetics are listed in Chapter II, n. 18. The best primary account of Palacký's philosophy of history, especially Czech history, is in the Introduction to the *Dějiny* (*DNČ*, I¹, 3-19). There is an abbreviated English translation of this by M. Weatherall, "The Mainspring of Czech History", *Central European Observer* (London), N. S., XIX (1942), 203. Various secondary accounts are: Fischer, I, 115-206; Chaloupecký, *DNČ 1939*, VI, 671-682; Milan Machovec, *František Palacký a česká filosofie* (Prague, 1961), *passim*, esp. 101-117; Jaroslav Werstadt, "The Philosophy of Czech History", *SR*, III, No. 9 (March, 1925), 533-546, repeated in greater detail in his *Odkazy dějin a dějepisců* (Prague, 1948), 15-21; the long, old, but still basic study by Josef Kalousek, "O vůdčích myšlenkách v historickém díle Palackého", *Památník 1898*, 177-232; Milena Jetmarová, "Filosofie Palackého", in Jiřina Popelová-Otáhalová and Karel Kosík, eds., *Filosofie v dějinách českého národa* (Prague, 1958), 135-149; Jetmarová, "Palackého filosofie dějin, její geneze a význam", *Acta universitatis Carolinae, Series philosophica et historica*, No. III (1958), 23-78, largely duplicated in her *František Palacký* (Prague, 1961), 53-106; and two brief sketches in English by Hans Kohn: *Not by Arms Alone: Essays on Our Time* (Cambridge, Mass., 1940), 65-83; and "The

interest is his central concept of *božnost* (*Gottartigkeit*, deiformity) as the final though unattainable goal of human life (unattainable because of the material element in man). Palacký defined *božnost* simultaneously as "kinship and likeness to God" and "the highest humanity". A "spark of divinity" exists in every man, urging him to strive through every means – reason, the will, feeling, imagination – toward many-sided perfection, toward ideas of absolute freedom, absolute good, absolute truth, and absolute beauty, i.e., toward likeness to God. This unending human progress in an infinite number of degrees toward "deiformity" forms the content of all history, whether it be the history of individuals or of all mankind. Czech scholars have outdone themselves in studying this concept. They have located its first appearance in Palacký's works at various times between 1817 and 1827. They have debated whether it is religious and theocentric or secular and anthropocentric in nature, a transcendental or an immanent state.[19] And they have attributed its origin, directly or indirectly, in whole or part, to a dismaying variety of sources: to Kant, Plato, and the Stoics, Schiller, Comenius, Thomas Aquinas (*via* Francis Bacon), Bacon (*via* Hugh Blair), Schelling, the Bible, Hus, the Czech Brethren, Friedrich von Schlegel, Hegel, Herder, Mme. de Staël, Jacob Fries, Friedrich Jacobi, Fichte, and others.[20]

Historical Roots of Czech Democracy", in Robert J. Kerner, ed., *Czechoslovakia* (Berkeley and Los Angeles, 1949), 91-105. The vast secondary literature is listed and discussed in Machovec, 6-19; and in Oldřich Králík, "Palackého božné doby", in *Tři studie*, ed. František Kutnar, 43-66; and most extensively utilized by Fischer.
[19] The chief supporter of the religious interpretation is Masaryk (see Chapter VI). The feasibility of both interpretations was first raised by Mirko Novák, "Palacký filosof a estetik", *Česká mysl*, XXXIV (1938), 227-245. The anthropocentric view is expounded very convincingly by J. M. Lochman, "Palackého božnost", *Křesťanská revue*, XIV (1947), 298-302. In recent times he has been seconded especially by the Marxists, who liken the concept to the materialistic and socialistic humanism of Feuerbach: Ladislav Rieger, "Poznámky k Palackého filosofii dějin lidstva", in *Zdeňku Nejedlému Československá Akademie Věd* (Prague, 1953), 437-449; and Machovec, 60-61. Fischer, II, 170-171, seeks to reconcile the two interpretations.
[20] On the influence of Kant: Leander Čech, "Palacký jako filosof", *Osvěta*, XV (1885), Pt. II, 1053-1073; also his "Palacký a Kant", *ČMM*, XXII (1898), 105-118, 221-233; and his "Palacký jako aesthetik", *Památník 1898*, 391-442; Plato and the Stoics (esp. Cicero and Seneca): Jaroslav Ludvíkovský, "Platonsko-stoický prvek v Palackého idei božnosti", *Listy filologické*, LXVIII (1941), 232-241; Schiller: Jan Patočka, "Idea božnosti v Palackého 'Krásovědě' ", *Křesťanská revue*, XXIII (1956), 118-123; and his "Filosofie dějin v Palackého 'Krásovědě' ", *ibid.*, 86-91; Comenius: F. M. Bartoš, "Palackého božnost a Komenský", *Národní kultura*, IV (1925), 57-70; Aquinas: Josef Pospíšil, "Hlavní principy krásovědy Františka Palackého se zřetelem k nauce svatého Tomáše Aquinského", *Hlídka*, III (1898),

Palacký's God is a Deist God who does not intervene directly in history but acts through natural laws. Progress toward *božnost* depends on the working of the "natural law of polarity", the eternal conflict between spiritual and material forces which pervades the universe and the source of movement in history. In this conflict neither side is ever completely victorious (although as an idealist Palacký believes that spiritual and moral forces must ultimately triumph and as an historian claims to see evidence of the progress of the human spirit throughout recorded history), but this is fortunate, for both are necessary and divinely-instituted for human progress. The spirit of man gains strength through opposition and sacrifice; uniformity means spiritual death. This is as true for individuals as for nations. However, it is the latter which, as carriers of eternal ideas and principles, are the most important historical agents. Indeed, a nation's worth lies in the worth of the idea it represents and advances, in its contribution to human progress. Consequently, a small nation can equal and surpass others far larger and stronger.[21] Palacký's "natural law of polarity" raises certain questions. Its roots have commonly been sought in Schelling [22] and Hegel. The influence of the latter has been much debated, however, for it cannot be proved that Palacký ever studied his philosophy. Heidler, the deepest student of the issue, is careful to state only that "Palacký might have been under the influence of Hegelianism" and that he probably "imbibed it from the atmosphere around him".[23] Josef Pfitzner, a Sudeten German historian, believes that the chief intermediary between Hegel and Palacký was Heinrich Luden, a pronounced Hegelian.[24] The Hege-

---

350 ff.; Bacon: Otakar Hostinský, "Fr. Palackého esthetické studie, 1816-1821", *Památník 1898*, 367-390; and Kalousek, *Památník 1898*, 177-232; Schelling: František Fajfr, "Měl Hegel vliv na českou literaturu?", *Česká mysl*, XXVIII (1932); Fries: Ladislav Rieger, "Kant a česká filosofie", *Česká mysl*, XXIX (1933), 148-161; the Czech Brethren and Herder: Masaryk's writings in general.

[21] In addition to being the custodian of an individual idea, a "nation" has other distinguishing features. Palacký conceived of it as a distinct social unit embracing all social classes, bound together by a common culture (religion, language, customs) and by certain subjective elements, especially a sense of historical continuity with the past and a strong feeling of "national consciousness". See František Kutnar, "Palackého pojetí společnosti, národa, a státu" [Palacký on Society, Nation, and State], in *Tři studie*, 7-42, esp. 23-32.

[22] Kalousek, *Památník 1898*, 192, n. 39.

[23] Jan Heidler, "O vlivu hegelismu na filosofii dějin a na politický programm Františka Palackého", *ČČH*, XVII (1911), 4, 166. He also believes that Hegelianism had more influence on Palacký's political program than on his historical philosophy (pp. 160-165).

[24] "Heinrich Luden und František Palacký", *HZ*, CXLI (1930), 92-94.

lian influence, if accepted, displays itself primarily in method, in the use of the dialectic. This presents further problems. Authorities disagree as to whether Palacký envisioned a higher synthesis of the two opposing forces or only an unending, mutually-beneficial antithesis, perhaps on an ever-rising level. Certainly such a synthesis is never clearly described either in his general statement of the theory or in his specific application of it to Bohemian history (see below). Perhaps a majority of the students of the problem reject the idea of synthesis, but some scholars have stated that such syntheses are clearly implied and have formulated them for both cases. Thus Václav Chaloupecký states that the synthesis of the Czech-German and Catholic-Protestant antitheses in Bohemian history (see below) is to be "a higher idea, the idea of national conciliation and toleration".[25] Milan Machovec agrees, citing Palacký's own words, that it is the function of the Czech nation "to serve as a bridge between Germandom and Slavdom, between eastern and western Europe in general".[26] Rudolf Urbánek, on the other hand, vigorously denies that Palacký contemplated such a synthesis, because it would involve condoning the disappearance of the Hussites and even the Czechs, which he did not desire.[27] When Palacký himself applied the polarity principle to contemporary politics, the desire for synthesis was more apparent. Since the seventeenth century, he claimed, religious conflict had been supplanted throughout the world by a struggle between the ideas of "nationality" and "world centralization", both the products of the great progress of science and technology. As the synthesis of this rivalry, Palacký expected that nationalities would first seek their own unification and then, for the sake of security, voluntarily merge on an equalitarian basis in new federalistic unions with strong central governments. He specifically applied this theory to the Habsburg empire in his *Idea státu rakouského* (1865).[28]

When applied specifically to Czech history, Palacký's philosophy gains in clarity. Throughout the history of Bohemia, he claimed, the "law of polarity" manifests itself chiefly in a struggle between Slavdom

---

[25] *DNČ 1939*, VI, 674.
[26] Pp. 108, 122. See also Fischer, II, 42, 193-197; and Heidler, *ČČH*, XVII, 157.
[27] *Památník Palackého 1926*, 33. See also Karel Kosík's detailed, Marxist explanation as to why Palacký's "law of polarity" could not mature into a genuine dialectical process ("the algebra of revolution") but remained merely a "law of equilibrium" between two opposing forces. *Česká radikální demokracie: Příspěvek k dějinám názorových sporů v české společnosti 19. století* (Prague, 1958), 426-430.
[28] See František Kutnar, *Tři studie*, 32-36.

and Germandom.[29] This conflict stems from an original difference in national characters. The Germans (like the Romans, Huns, Avars, Mongols, Tartars, and Turks) made their first appearance in history as rapacious aggressors and conquerors (*Räubervölker*, later softened to *Raubvölker*). The Slavs (like the Jews and Greeks) were peaceful, sensitive, religious, and industrious people, unskilled in warfare and disinterested in ruling over others. The ancient Slavic communities enjoyed a rough democracy and legal equality; but in primitive German society, from the very beginning, a privileged military caste ruled over a mass of slaves and serfs (with the adoption of Roman law, this system was easily reshaped into formal feudalism).[30] The clash between these two disparate cultures reached epic proportions in the area of their closest proximity, on the classic battleground of Bohemia and Moravia:

The chief content and basic feature of the whole history of Bohemia-Moravia is . . . the continual association and conflict of Slavdom with Romandom and Germandom . . .; and as Romandom did not reach the Slavs directly, but almost entirely through the mediation of Germandom, one may therefore say that Czech history is based chiefly on a conflict with Germandom, that is, on the acceptance and rejection of German customs and laws by the Czechs. . . .
[It is] a struggle waged not only on the borders but in the interior of Bohemia, not only against foreigners but among native inhabitants, not only with sword and shield but with spirit and word, laws and customs, openly

[29]   According to Fischer (I, 99-100), the Czech-German antithesis as the key to Bohemian history first appears in Palacký's writings in an unpublished collection of reading notes made in Pressburg in 1819. It is repeated next in 1822, in his long literary review, "An- und Aussichten der böhmischen Sprache und Literatur vor 50 Jahren", written for the *Wiener Jahrbücher der Literatur* (but rejected by the censor and first printed in 1874 in *Gedenk.*, 19-47; Czech translation in *Spisy drobné*, III, 489-509), and in his unpublished "Geschichte der schönen Redekünste bei den Böhmen" (1825-1827). See the detailed description and analysis of the "Aussichten" by Luboš Holý, "Komentář k stati Františka Palackého: Rozhledy a výhledy české řeči a literatury z roku 1822", *Slovesná věda*, III (1948-49), Nos. 1-4, pp. 12-20. A parallel German-Czech edition of the "Redekünste" is scheduled in Prague in late 1968.
[30]   See *Geschichte des Hussitenthums*, 74-89. This conception of "national character", stressed more in the Czech version of the *History* than in the German one, owes much to Palacký's reading of the works of Lelewel, Maciejowski, Rousseau, and especially his "glorious priest of humanity", Herder, reinforced by the testimony of the forged "Manuscripts" and Palacký's own unhappy impressions of the contemporary Germans in the Habsburg empire and the Germanies. Interestingly, Palacký's view of the ancient Slavs was not always so favorable. In the 1830's he was quite critical of the efforts of Kollár and others to idealize them, writing in 1834 to Vinařický: "The Slavs live by the same right on the Elbe as the Germans on the Rhine: the right of the sword, and more than a thousand years of occupation." Quoted in Chaloupecký, *František Palacký*, 158.

and covertly, with enlightened zeal and blind passion, leading not only to victory or subjection but also to reconciliation.[31]

In accord with his general philosophy, Palacký did not consider this struggle, this "red thread stretching for a thousand years through Bohemian history", exclusively in negative terms, even though the less numerous and less developed Czechs were generally on the defensive. Slav democracy and lack of aggressiveness too often degenerated into capricious disunity and stubborn parochialism. In order to save themselves before the German onslaught, the Czechs were forced to adopt useful strains of their neighbor's culture and to imitate some of his qualities, to accept elements of the Germans' authoritarian form of government and to adopt Christianity. They thus disciplined themselves, overcame their own tendency toward anarchy, and preserved and improved their existence (other western Slavic tribes refused to do so and disappeared). Nevertheless, Germans – farmers, hunters, monks – and German material and spiritual culture continued to filter into the country during the "Old Period" of Czech history (to 1403).[32] In the thirteenth century, under the Přemyslids (especially Přemysl Otakar II), German feudalism was introduced and gained ground under the Luxemburgs in the fourteenth. This was met in the "Central Period" (1403-1627) by a Slavic and democratic reaction in the Hussite Revolution. But at the battle of Lipany (1434), where the aristocratic and moderate Hussite-Catholic coalition defeated the radical Taborites, domestic feudal forces crushed the democratic ones, remnants of which took refuge with the Czech Brethren. Complete feudalization, temporarily delayed by the popular "Hussite King", George of Poděbrady, was accomplished late in the fifteenth century under the weak Jagellonians. Driven into hereditary serfdom, the great peasant masses were alienated from their privileged masters, making the defeat of the latter at the battle of White Mountain (1620) a foregone conclusion. In 1627, with the Renewed Land Ordinance of Ferdinand II and the exiling of the Utraquists, the "New Period" of Czech history began, with the country Germanized, Catholicized, and subject to the hereditary absolutism of the Habsburgs.[33]

---

[31] DNČ, I¹, 12-13.
[32] There is a detailed breakdown of Palacký's three periods of Czech history in Fischer, I, 164-206.
[33] Since the *History* ends with 1526, Palacký's views on Czech history after that date must be assembled from remarks in minor and occasional works. They are not always consistent. The voluntary union of Bohemia with neighboring territories in the Habsburg monarchy in 1526 he viewed with favor, believing that it eliminated

Palacký believed that in the "Central Period", especially in the Hussite era, the Czech nation had attained its highest historical significance.[34] In addition to its national and social-political features, sketched above, the Hussite movement was also, of course, a religious revolution.[35] Here, too, the "polarity" principle was at work. According to Palacký, all thought, including religious thought, is activated by external authority or internal conscience and reason. The original teachings of Christ, especially the injunctions to love God above all else and one's fellows as oneself, were the highest manifestations of reason. But the Catholic hierarchy, established to propagate these teachings, gradually usurped complete authority of its own, declaring itself the embodiment of the Holy Ghost and the custodian of all oral and written tradition, rejecting individual recourse to Holy Writ as superfluous, and using

---

centuries of warfare between them and protected them from being forcibly absorbed by larger nations. Sometimes he attributed the defeat at White Mountain to political, religious, and moral debasement on the part of the Czechs, of which the Pope and the Habsburgs took advantage. At other times he saw it as part of a European-wide phenomenon, the steady growth of absolutism and political centralization at the expense of feudalism, and thus beyond Czech control. He viewed with horror the material and human devastation of the Thirty Years' War and the cultural barbarism of the period of the Counter-Reformation (*Temno*, darkness). He praised the enlightened reforms of Maria Theresa and Joseph II; ultimately, however, Joseph's centralizing and Germanizing efforts provoked the Czech National Revival as a domestic reaction, he sometimes believed. At other times, he saw the Revival rather as the result of the incursions into Bohemia of the Enlightenment and the French Revolution (which themselves embodied many of the ideas of the Czech Reformation, he believed, and thus provided a bridge between the latter period and the Revival period). The Revival itself he regarded primarily as a linguistic-literary phenomenon. See Fischer, I, 191-206; II, 190-192; Kalousek, *Památník 1898*, 225; and Jaroslav Charvát, *Z dějin národu českého* (Prague, 1957), 24-25.

[34] Palacký's unusual personal interest in Hussite history, a topic long neglected when he took it up, has often been explained by the fact that he spent his childhood in a region dominated by the faith of the Czech Brethren. Both Fischer (I, 99) and Králík (*Tři studie*, 151-153) trace the first mention of this interest in his writings to 1817. The latter believes that Palacký was much influenced by the reports of his friends at Jena, who had witnessed the stirring Luther celebrations at the *Wartburgfest* in that year, and by his own identification of the Hussite period as the "deiform period" of the Czech nation (the period when it was closest to deiformity). (Králík identifies Palacký's own "deiform period" as the years 1818-1819.) A comprehensive, though Marxist-oriented survey of Czech attitudes toward Hus and the Hussite Revolution from Hus's own day to the present is Milan Machovec, *Husovo učení a význam v tradici českého národa* (Prague, 1953). On the attitudes of Palacký's predecessors, see Werstadt, *SR*, III, No. 9, 536-538; also his *Odkazy dějin a dějepisců*, 9-15, 129-148; and Fischer, II, 198-200.

[35] Perhaps Palacký's own best characterization of the Hussites in this sense is in the *Geschichte des Hussitenthums*, 59-66, 158-160 (parts translated into English in Lützow, *Historians*, 103-104).

force against beliefs it considered unorthodox. However, the principles
of reason and authority were both instituted by Providence; their competition is necessary not only for the preservation and unity of the
Church, but for the spiritual progress and salvation of the individual
soul as well. It was the great merit of the Hussites, as the first "Protes-
tants", to redress the balance, to oppose human reason and Holy Writ
to hierarchical authority and abstract dogmas. In so doing, they not
only advanced the cause of religious toleration but helped to regenerate
the Christian Church itself. Hus, not Luther, was the author and
founder of "Protestantism", and the Hussite, not the Lutheran, was the
first great attempt at a Christian reformation.[36] The Taborites and the
Bohemian Brethren had developed the Protestant teachings fully, long
before Luther and Calvin, and the successful Hussite defense made the
Catholic Church reluctant to try full-scale repression again against the
Swiss and German reformations. Palacký was, of course, well aware of
the long, continuous series of reformers who had opposed the Church
hierarchy since its very beginnings on the grounds of Holy Writ and
individual conscience. The Hussite Revolution was unique, however,
in its strength and breadth, its involvement of an entire nation, and its
unconquerability. As such, the Hussites had struck a resounding blow
at the claims of the medieval Church to supreme world authority, a
blow which had its echo in the famous plan of the "Hussite King",
George of Poděbrady, for an international league of secular rulers, a
European states system free of papal interference. Further, the Hussite
Wars were the first great international conflict over spiritual matters,
matters of conscience, ideas, and the first great victory of individual
freedom over the all-leveling authority of the Middle Ages. If the
Hussite movement ultimately failed, it was because it had betrayed its
own principles, had deteriorated into spiritual parochialism and theological squabbling, had lost its unity and great moral supremacy over
its enemies, and had alienated itself from the spiritual needs of the
common people. But for one brief moment in the fifteenth century, its
heroic courage and dedication had pushed the small Czech nation to
the very forefront of European civilization and had forever guaranteed
it an honored place in the history of human enlightenment. "We were
and are no longer", wrote Palacký at twenty-five. "But our fall was the
fall of a hero who dies for right and truth. Though our former life has
disappeared in time, it has not disappeared in eternity – it gleams and

---

[36] See Palacký's criticism of Ranke for ignoring the Hussite achievement, in
Geschichte des Hussitenthums, 160.

will always gleam as a model and mirror as long as humanity exists." [37]

The question may be asked, which of the two motivations, the national or the religious, did Palacký consider more important in the Hussite movement? (Most authorities agree that the social-political aspect – democracy vs. feudalism – always remained a minor one to him.) Many have thought that in the third volume of the German edition (1845-1854) and of the first Czech edition (1850-1851), he gave precedence to the antagonism of the two nationalities. After the polemic with Höfler, who used this characterization to detract from the significance of the movement, Palacký may have changed his mind. In the revised Czech edition (Volume III, 1870-1872), he seems to stress the religious motives – only after the Czechs were branded a nation of heretics did they develop a sense of national solidarity. The difference between editions displays itself chiefly in various expressions, not in significant changes in content or organization. After a careful re-examination of the latter, Rudolf Urbánek concluded that Palacký did not reverse himself – that the emphasis on the nationality conflict is indeed strong in all editions but that it is always subordinate to the religious one, though the latter may have been strengthened after the Höfler criticisms.[38] Some authorities have remained unconvinced. Fischer believes that Palacký did shift the emphasis but that the change is unimportant: both Czech-German and Protestant-Catholic antitheses are simply aspects of the third, of democracy vs. aristocracy.[39] It is not impossible that Palacký himself never quite made up his mind.

Enough has already been said about the attempts to identify with precision the origins of the various segments of Palacký's philosophy to indicate how unsatisfactory the results of such investigations have been.[40]

---

[37]   Palacký to Ondřej Rudelbach, January 26, 1824 (book dedication), in Karel Hikl, *Listy českého probuzení* (Prague, 1920), 82.
[38]   *Památník Palackého 1926*, 31-37.
[39]   I, 171-172; II, 189-190.
[40]   The most painstaking attempt is that of Fischer, II, 9-158, who has traced all important literary leads, identified them, and attempted to determine what Palacký drew from each. More recently, Marxist scholars in Czechoslovakia have somewhat simplified the question of influences. They agree that Palacký was an eclectic who drew upon "a sort of mutual-aid company of authorities, supporting and corroborating one another". (Králík, in *Tři studie*, 274.) What determined his principle of selection, however (i.e., the overriding influence upon his philosophy of history), was his desire and need to formulate an ideology that would support the political and cultural aspirations of the Czech liberal bourgeoisie in the early nineteenth century. In addition to Králík's study, see, for example: Jetmarová, *Acta universitatis Carolinae*, III, 23-78; Machovec, *passim*; and Rieger, in *Zdeňku Nejedlému ČSAV*, 444.

One inclines toward Pfitzner's view that many authors mentioned by young Palacký "remained only names for him, and to wish to determine their influence on his later life-work would be a futile effort".[41] An especially futile and scarcely disinterested facet of the business has been the attempt to establish the relative weight and chronological precedence of various national influences on Palacký's development, especially English and German influences (the former quite rare in the Bohemian environment), above all in the crucial years at Pressburg. This forms part of the larger debate over the extent of German influence on the beginnings of the Czech National Revival and on Czech culture in general. For example, Otakar Vočadlo claims: "It is time to discard the dogma of Palacký's indebtedness to Germany. ... In the most important period of his life, when his character was being moulded and his future career finally determined, it seems that English influences play a decisive part – in poetry, aesthetics, and even politics no less than in history." [42] His evidence is not entirely convincing, however. He points out that Palacký read English authors before German ones, that he generally resented German dominance over Czech culture, that he used the typically English expression "fair play" in dealing with the Austrian Germans, etc.[43] He is given able support by Simeon Potter who, pointing to the influence of Blair, Bolingbroke, Gibbon, and Robertson, states that "Palacký learned to comprehend history in a broad, modern, and philosophical spirit first of all from the English".[44] Those Germans who have not tried to detract from Palacký's stature have been eager to present him as the prototype of a Czech imbued with German culture and to accuse him of "ingratitude to his German heritage". In Josef Pfitzner's view, "The exaggerated emphasis on English influences is certainly not correct. Much more came to Palacký from German culture, by far the greatest number of and most important elements." [45] In reviewing the *Geschichte von Böhmen* in 1843, the Silesian historian, Ludwig Häusser, insisted: "The author is ... the offspring of German training. ... We see

---

[41] *HZ*, CXLI, 96.
[42] "English Influences upon Palacký", *SR*, III, No. 9 (March, 1925), 548, 550, 552.
[43] In his *V zajetí babylonském* (Prague, 1924), 45, Vočadlo even claimed a direct connection between Palacký and Gladstone because of the similarity of their views on the preservation of Austria as a bulwark against Russia, though there is no evidence to support this.
[44] "Palacký a anglické písemnictví", *ČMM*, LIII (1929), 131. Together, the Vočadlo and Potter articles present a patiently-assembled record of all of Palacký's contacts with English culture.
[45] *HZ*, CXLI, 96.

everywhere only the fruit of German studies, the product of German historical art." [46] The Germans argue that Palacký read more German than English works in his formative period, that in Pressburg his social and intellectual contacts were mostly with persons who had studied or lived for significant periods in Germany, and that (as he himself admitted) his contacts with English culture were largely severed after 1823.[47] According to Pfitzner, the greatest and most enduring influence of all on Palacký was Heinrich Luden ('Luden's genius hovered over the workroom of the greatest of Czech historians" [48]). As "proof" he cites Palacký's flattering references to him ("one of the most discerning historical researchers of our time", "one of the most thoughtful of German historians") and his frequent citation of Luden's works in his *History*. Palacký's own simple remarks [49] do not point conclusively in the direction of either nationality, English or German, though he specifically denied that he was the product of a predominantly German education, claiming that he was mostly self-taught and an eclectic.[50] If a decision must be made, and judging simply from the nature of the significant works Palacký acknowledged reading in each language, one is inclined to say that the English had more to do with his views on historical method and the Germans with his philosophy of history, and that both combined to turn him toward history as a vocation.[51]

[46] Quoted (and concurred in) by Colmar Grünhagen, "Fr. Palacký: Ein deutscher Historiker wider Willen", *Preussische Jahrbücher*, XXVIII (1871), 240. A similar judgment is given by Robert von Zimmermann, "Palacký", *Památník 1898*, 41-44; and, more colorfully, by Friedrich Engels, writing under Marx's name in the *New York Tribune*, March 5, 1852: "The chief champion of the Tschechian nationality, Professor Palacký, is himself nothing but a learned German run mad, who even now cannot speak the Tschechian language correctly and without foreign accent."
[47] However, he continued to read and to review in the Museum journals such English and American periodicals as the *Edinburgh Review*, the *North American Review*, the *Foreign Quarterly Review*, and the *British and Foreign Review*.
[48] *HZ*, CXLI, 90.
[49] One quotation is especially used as evidence by both sides: "I became fond of historical learning only later, having read Robertson's writings and Bolingbroke's meditation on history.... From the English and then from the German Luden I learned to look upon history in a philosophical and political spirit." "Každodenníček", January 1, 1820, *Kor. a záp.*, I, 59.
[50] *ZBG*, 174-176.
[51] Fischer (II, 155-158) accepts the Germans as the middlemen of general culture to Palacký, but insists that Palacký did not come under the influence of any German "school" and that he was an eclectic, taking whatever suited his needs. Válka (*Sborník prací ... Brněnské university*) suggests still another, heretofore unexplored national influence upon Palacký's theory and philosophy of history – the French historians of the Restoration period (Guizot, Thierry), whose works Palacký knew and valued.

Which had the greater share in shaping Palacký's *History* – his clinical theory of historiography or his highly personalized philosophy of history? Palacký himself averred that "he had never dared go further than definite historical sources, critically examined, had permitted him to go".[52] It is true that the philosophy of history dictates the periodization of the work, and that its traces appear more clearly in some parts (e.g., Volumes I, III, and IV) than in others, but it never makes its appearance blatantly in the detailed exposition itself. Many scholars, usually historians (such as Josef Pekař), claim that the philosophy of history appears mainly in various introductions (to Volumes I, Part I; III, Part I; and IV, Part II) and in numerous inserted aphorisms and minor reflections, but that Palacký never forces his empirical findings into a preconceived pattern. This view is supported by the fact that, although all or part of the philosophy of history has been rejected by subsequent Czech historians (especially the Goll school), the *History* still maintains much of its factual validity. Two authorities, both professional philosophers, insist that the work is permeated by the philosophy of history and that Palacký employed the "law of polarity", admittedly a flexible tool, to solve many specific minor problems. They add, however, that he usually brought it into play only when empirical evidence supported it or did not controvert it.[53] Any final conclusion is ruled out, of course, by the difficulty of confidently attributing any specific erroneous conclusion either to the influence of the philosophy of history or to legitimate historical shortcomings – an inadequacy of sources, faulty reasoning, or involuntary personal bias.[54]

Palacký's was the first comprehensive philosophy of Czech history, and until the advent of the Marxists the only one. From the foregoing it is apparent that, judged rigorously by the established standards of the discipline, he was not particularly successful as a practicing philosopher ("perhaps", adds Heidler somewhat maliciously, "precisely because he was such an excellent historian!"). Though interesting, his philosophy of history is incomplete, often vague, and sometimes even inconsistent. Nevertheless, it is an excellent example of "nationalist messianism" and well qualifies Palacký for the title of "national prophet", to use the

---

[52] *DNČ*, V², Preface (March 3, 1867), ix.

[53] Fischer, II, 175-189; Machovec, 62, 103, 110-111; and the latter's "Místo filosofie v dějepisném díle Františka Palackého", *Acta universitatis Carolinae, Series philosophica et historica*, No. II (1958), 213-234; and his *Husovo učení*, 305. See also Válka, *Sborník ... Brněnské university*, 83.

[54] Palacký's personal biases, especially the ethnic, political, religious, and philosophical ones, are neatly summarized by Werstadt in *Odkazy*, 20-21.

familiar terms of Hans Kohn.[55] Through it, Palacký gave Czech nationalism a new, positive content and a firm Western, liberal, and humanitarian foundation. He also solved the problem of finding a justification for the continued existence of a small nation. "Through [Palacký] Czech history became of importance for the history of Europe, the Czech question a universal question. . . . The Czechs found their place in modern Europe on the side of the great and progressive democratic currents and peoples." [56] A source of popular inspiration to the Czechs from Palacký's day to this, the philosophy of history, together with his historical working program and the patiently-assembled pages of the *History*, also constituted Palacký's great legacy to the generations of historians who followed him.

[55] The "national prophets" developed "a philosophy of history and society in the center of which stood their own nation and the principle which was to sum up its idea and faith". Hans Kohn, *Prophets and Peoples: Studies in Nineteenth Century Nationalism* (New York, 1961), 11. Their philosophy was characterized by "nationalist pride, often cloaked in humility and grounded in real or imaginary sufferings and offenses, . . . [claiming] to serve the cause of universal peace and justice." Kohn, *Reflections on Modern History* (Princeton, New Jersey, 1963), 134.
[56] Kohn, *Not by Arms Alone*, 81. Machovec, *František Palacký a česká filosofie*, 116, believes that the tradition of freedom of conscience and refusal of blind obedience to authority which stemmed from Palacký's *History* accounts for the lack of appeal of fascism for the Czech intelligentsia in the twentieth century.

THE PALACKÝ LEGACY

It is certain that with the year 1526 my work is ended, but not at all completed . . . . For the natural law of progress rules in historiography as in all things human . . . . I am not ashamed to admit that even in my old age I still learn more and more each day . . . . Let fresh forces . . . conduct the work to its necessary end. They will have to contend with other, but scarcely lesser difficulties than I did. I only wish from the depths of my soul . . . that our beloved nation, in all times so heavily tried above all others, may as soon as possible receive a faithful mirror of all its past for its instruction, remembrance, and strengthening, . . . that it may always stride along the paths of truth and right, neither glorying in its success nor ever losing its courage in adversity.

> Palacký, *DNČ*, V², Preface (March 3, 1867), vii, lx-x.

Palacký's original commission from the Bohemian Estates in 1831 had called for a complete history of Bohemia, from the earliest times to the present, in four or five volumes, a charge he acknowledged and accepted in the introduction to the first volume of the *Geschichte von Böhmen*.[1] But as decades passed and the *History* slowly took shape, the suspicion grew in him that he would not accomplish this and that he would have to find a continuator. We do not know precisely when he arrived at this decision, however. In 1850 he still envisioned the possibility of reaching 1627, perhaps even further.[2] The first public hint that he was considering an earlier terminus, 1526, appeared in his brief preface to the second edition of Volume I (written December 18, 1861) where, calling attention to his advancing age and the incomplete state of what he had already written, he expressed the hope that "perhaps someone else will

---

[1] *Geschichte von Böhmen*, I (1836), v.
[2] In the introduction to the first edition of Volume III, Part I, of the *Dějiny*, cited in Rudolf Urbánek, *Památník Palackého 1926*, 29.

be able to continue the work I have begun".[3] By July of the following year he had definitely made up his mind, announcing his decision to the Estates and requesting the selection and appointment of a successor.[4] He gave various reasons:

I have dedicated my activity almost exclusively to the study of Bohemian history for nearly forty full years. I am convinced that I have not been untrue for a moment to this high duty of my life and that I have always devoted to it all the physical and spiritual strength at my disposal. But in the meantime I have grown old, my strength is waning, my faculties are becoming dull and weak, and my memory still holds good only for the old historical data, while it more and more refuses to have anything to do with large new acquisitions.[5]

But "the peculiar circumstances connected with the sources of our history" were also involved: "For while the Bohemian historian ... must struggle before 1526 with a lack of necessary sources and information, after 1526 he is faced with a problem of a different sort, with a surplus of them." [6] To master this newer material would require "fresh, young strength for a long series of years". As for himself, he felt it important to complete and correct what he had already written in the light of his own progressively greater knowledge and insight. This decision and its reasons were accepted by the Estates and made public in the prefaces to the two parts of Volume V in 1864 and 1867.[7]

In selecting a successor, Palacký turned first to his pupils and as-

---

[3] *DNČ*, I¹, lix-lx. As late as 1860, however, Palacký was apparently still not sure that 1526 would be the terminal date of his own writing. On October 19, 1860, he wrote to Droysen that he had definitely given up the intention of going past the battle of Mohács and that he would probably entrust a further continuation to Anton Gindely. Hübner, ed., *Johann Gustav Droysen Briefwechsel*, II, 697. But on November 26, Gindely wrote to Palacký: "As long as you feel the strength to work, it would be vain effort [for me] to turn to Bohemian history in the sixteenth century. After ending your history with 1526, you will surely feel the urge to advance further, and I do not intend to begin save where you end." Quoted in Kamil Krofta, "Palacký a Gindely", *ČČH*, XVIII (1912), 290.
[4] *ZBG*, 139-140.
[5] *Ibid.*, 140.
[6] *Dějiny*, V¹, Preface (November 6, 1864), in *DNČ*, V¹, x.
[7] *DNČ*, V¹, v-xii; V², iii-x. Palacký had already announced to a Polish correspondent, J. Chociszewski, in late 1863, that his own writing would end with 1526, that Anton Gindely would carry on from there, and that Palacký himself would turn to a revision of the entire work. Palacký to Chociszewski, December 26, 1863, *LAPNP*, Palacký collection, sign. 11 C 11 (copy). Two months before his death, Palacký was still contemplating revision of his work, though, with his eyes failing, he had abandoned the hope of doing it properly. See Palacký to Louis Leger, March 17, 1876, *LAPNP*, Leger collection, sign. 20 P 71 (original); Palacký collection, sign. 11 C 11 (copy).

sistants – Václav Vladivoj Tomek (1818-1905), Karel Jaromír Erben (1811-1870), Josef Emler (1836-1899), and Josef Kalousek (1838-1915).[8] Apparently he originally decided on Tomek as the most promising and then, for various reasons, came to consider him unsuitable. Tomek first met Palacký as tutor to his two children, Jan and Marie, in 1839. He stayed on until about 1850, not only as Palacký's trusted historical assistant but as his devoted political co-worker in 1848-1849, sharing his liberal views and taking part with him in the unsuccessful imperial constitutional assemblies in Vienna and Kremsier. During this time the two men were very close. Palacký sought out various writing commissions and other salaried occupations for Tomek, including a new opening in history at Prague University and a position with the Prague magistracy involving care of the city archive and the writing of a history of Prague. In 1846-1847, when the Executive Committee of the Bohemian Estates briefly contemplated appointing an official assistant to their Historiographer, Palacký recommended Tomek most strongly for the post, adding that "under present conditions, he would probably also be the best qualified to finish the historical work I have begun, in case of my early death".[9] But with the coming of the Bach Reaction in 1851, Tomek's political convictions changed, seemingly overnight, and alien-

[8] Tomek and Kalousek, together with Gindely, Antonín Rezek (1853-1910), and Bohuš Rieger (1857-1907), are the subject of a special study by Jaroslav Werstadt, "Politické dějepisectví devatenáctého století a jeho čeští představitelé", ČČH, XXVI (1920), 1-93. He labels them "Political Historians" and considers them a separate group situated between the preceding "Romantic Historians" (ca. 1830-1880) and the following "Positivistic Historians" (ca. 1880-1948) on the grounds that their historical labors had an especially close link with contemporary political conditions. This differentiation does not seem apt. (See also Fischer, Myšlenka a dílo, II, 215-217.) Many historians of all three groups were involved with the political issues of their day, and they often chose and developed their historical themes accordingly, the difference between individuals and groups in this respect being simply one of degree. This latter viewpoint is developed and illustrated, not wihout a certain German bias, by Richard Georg Plaschka, Von Palacký bis Pekař: Geschichtswissenschaft und Nationalbewusstsein bei den Tschechen (Graz-Köln, 1955).
[9] ZBG, 115-116; see also Krofta, ČČH, XVIII, 293-294. In his memoirs, Tomek insists that Palacký had intended him to be not merely his assistant but his "coadjutor" and successor. When the Estates ultimately balked in 1847 at appointing a "regular official" to assist Palacký, the frugal Palacký not only kept him on only as an ad hoc assistant but reduced his pay from six hundred to five hundred florins annually, in the mistaken belief that Tomek was to marry a wealthy woman. (Paměti, I, 227-228, 245-246, 324-325). Wrote Tomek: "Mr. Palacký, a great spirit in scholarship and in public life in general, was not sufficiently acquainted with the petty aspects of life." (Paměti, I, 249-250). Palacký even made deductions from Tomek's pay for the time the latter had spent in various assemblies in 1848! Tomek's contacts and historical co-labors with Palacký till 1862 are summarized in his "Styky mé s Palackým do roku 1862", Památník 1898, 61-93.

ated Palacký.[10] Appointed professor of Austrian history at the University of Prague, he became a staunch apologist for imperial loyalty, his historical views changing radically, too. Previously opposed (though himself a Catholic) to "ultramontanism" and "Habsburg despotism", he now claimed, like the Counter-Reformation historians before him, that Hus had seduced the Czech nation from its proper path to salvation and that the defeat at White Mountain and the rigors of the Counter-Reformation in Bohemia had been salutary correctives. His alienation from Palacký was increased in 1852 when he replaced the older man on the governing committee of the Bohemian Museum, from which the regime had had Palacký removed. Not even their mutual defense of the "Manuscripts" in 1859 nor the moderating of Tomek's historical and political views after 1860 managed to reconcile the two men fully again. Moreover, when the first volume of Tomek's classic *History of Prague* appeared in 1855, it was apparent that the project would be a lifetime undertaking and that Tomek himself might eventually need a continuator.[11] Palacký therefore turned elsewhere, to Anton Gindely.

Gindely (1829-1892), whose father was a Hungarian German and his mother Czech, received his Ph. D. from Prague University in 1852. After teaching at the university at Olomouc and the Czech *Realgymnasium* in Prague, he returned to his *alma mater* as a professor of Austrian history in 1862. From his earliest publication in 1854, he revealed himself as energetic and industrious, with a talent for mastering an abundance of source material and considerable literary ability. His interest in the history of the Czech Brethren and the Bohemian uprising of 1618 and his passion for archival research also made him the logical choice as Palacký's successor. But, as in the case of Tomek, there were certain obstacles. Like Tomek, Gindely was a Catholic, he preferred to write in German, and he was possessed of a "colorless Austrian nationality".[12] But, as Krofta has shown in his finely-detailed study, these drawbacks were less important than has often been believed, and

---

[10]   No explanation is offered for Tomek's weather-vane reversals save Werstadt's characterization of him as "something of a plebeian spirit, displaying itself in willing servitude and easy submissiveness to the spiritual and temporal authorities of this world". "Na okraj historického díla Tomkova", *Odkazy dějin a dějepisců* (Prague, 1948), 93.

[11]   *Dějepis města Prahy* (12 vols.; Prague, 1855-1901), to 1609. Tomek's exhaustive attention to detail and his avoidance of philosophical speculation have led some Czech historians, notably the Goll school, to rank him with Palacký as one of the founders of modern Czech historiography.

[12]   Says Werstadt, "Tomek is an Austrian-minded Czech, Gindely is an Austrian with Czech sympathies." *ČČH*, XXVI, 54.

Gindely was essentially in agreement with Palacký in his national, political, and religious outlook.[13] After a careful study of Gindely's works and correspondence, Krofta concluded, for example, that though Gindely was not a Czech his associations and researches had made him quite sympathetic to the Czech cause; that, though a devoted Austrian, he was a liberal who opposed absolutism and recognized the need for satisfying the demands of the non-ruling nationalities of the empire; and that, though a fervent Catholic, he personally admired the Bohemian Brethren and lamented the Church's use of force against the Hussites. He also shared Palacký's distrust of Prussia and his defense of the "Manuscripts".

The first contacts between the two came at the end of 1855 or the beginning of 1856, when Palacký permitted Gindely to consult a still-unpublished part of the *Dějiny* (Vol. IV, Part I) for his research on the first volume of his own *Geschichte der Böhmischen Brüder* (2 vols.; Prague, 1857-1858). In late 1859, while Palacký was in Nice, Gindely shared with Tomek in the proofreading of the second part of this volume (*ZBG*, 135). Krofta deduced that in the summer of that year, before Palacký's departure, Gindely had tentatively agreed to continue the *History* and Palacký had promised to provide Gindely with a livelihood by recommending him for the appointment as head of the newly-contemplated Archive of the Bohemian Kingdom.[14] Certainly from the end of 1860 Gindely was generally recognized as Palacký's successor. On July 15, 1862, Palacký requested the Estates to appoint an official archivist with the added function of eventually continuing his *History*,[15] submitting the names of both Tomek and Gindely as qualified candidates, but recommending the latter "because he is much younger . . .; he will devote a whole life exclusively to this task".[16] Palacký did not contemplate relinquishing the title and duties of Historiographer of the Bohemian Estates as long as his strength held out. However, in order to make his proposal more palatable to the Estates, he offered to contribute the extra six hundred florins which they had granted him annually since 1846 to pay his assistants and his travel expenses toward

[13] "Palacký a Gindely", *ČČH*, XVIII (1912), 275-320. See also Krofta's long biographical article, "Antonín Gindely", *Zprávy zemského archivu království českého*, IV (1915), 145-396, esp. 252-274, 292-395. Gindely's dual loyalty cost him dear: both Czechs and Germans distrusted him, and neither claimed him as their national historian.
[14] *ČČH*, XVIII, 287, 289.
[15] Palacký's proposal and its approval by the Estates are reprinted in *ZBG*, 139-143.
[16] *Ibid.*, 141.

the proposed archivist's annual salary of one thousand florins. The Executive Committee of the Estates accepted Palacký's proposal for the archivist-position, but, in recognition of his past services, gratefully rejected his proffered financial sacrifice. Gindely was provisionally appointed Archivist of the Kingdom of Bohemia on July 29, 1862.[17]

Despite these well-laid plans, Gindely did not really become Palacký's successor; his researches did not begin where Palacký's left off, and he himself gradually became estranged from Czech society. The causes are not completely clear. To be sure, Gindely was bound only by his personal promise to Palacký. The continuation of the *History* had not, after all, been made an official part of the Archivist's duties, although the Estates continued, at least tacitly and in practice, to recognize this as one of his functions. Moreover, Gindely had stipulated that he would first have to complete certain lengthy preliminary works of his own, including a history of the uprising of 1618 and the Thirty Years' War. Nevertheless, Krofta maintains that Gindely was sincere, that his personal associations with Palacký remained friendly until the latter's death, and that he did not consciously abandon his promise until about 1880. In that year the fourth volume of his *History of the Bohemian Uprising* [18] met with brutal treatment at the hands of Czech journalists, with talk of "this gypsy laying his unclean hands on the glorious pages of Czech history." [19] Two years later, when Prague University was divided into separate Czech and German universities, Gindely chose the latter and was henceforth lost to the Czech cause and to the *Dějiny*.

After Gindely, no further continuators were sought for the *Dějiny*, and it still remains an unfinished torso. Actually, as Jaroslav Goll pointed out, "a true completion of Palacký's work became impossible at the very moment when he himself gave it up".[20] Potential successors feared to measure themselves against Palacký's talent, and without his

[17] The post was definitely approved by the Estates in 1863, but debates over the function and organization of the archive, in which Palacký took some part, continued until 1869. See Borovička, *Zprávy zemského archivu*, IV, 3-20; and *Spisy drobné*, I, 269-273.

[18] *Dějiny českého povstání* (4 vols.; Prague, 1869-1880); also in German, *Geschichte des dreissigjährigen Krieges*, and in an abbreviated English translation by Andrew Ten Brook, *History of the Thirty Years' War* (2 vols.; New York, 1883).

[19] Quoted in Krofta, *ČČH*, XVIII, 320.

[20] "Palackého programm práce historické", *ČČH*, IV (1898), 4. But a good share of the responsibility must go to Goll himself, who stressed the study of the medieval, over the modern period and who rigidly refused to permit his students to attempt any surveys until many years of detailed research had thoroughly prepared the way for them (see below).

great inner resolution and the cohesion provided by his personal philosophy of history, any continuation of his work could only have been an external one.[21] The only historian who might conceivably be considered Palacký's successor was not a Czech, but a Frenchman, Ernest Denis (1849-1921). He first met Palacký in Prague in 1872, a twenty-three-year-old whose interest in Czech history had been kindled by the defeat of France by the "common enemy" in 1870.[22] During the succeeding three years he received friendly encouragement but scarcely formal training from Palacký. Nevertheless, his two works, covering the period from 1434 to 1900 – *La Fin de l'indépendance bohême* (2 vols.; Paris, 1890) and *La Bohême depuis la Montagne Blanche* (2 vols.; Paris, 1901-1903) – were indeed cut from the same cloth as Palacký's. Like Palacký, Denis believed that history ought to be of help to the present, to aid in achieving "greater freedom, justice, and humanity", and that an historian's chief attention should be directed toward "general spiritual movements".[23] Based heavily on Czech scholarship, and written from an idealistic, Protestant, and democratic point of view, the two books are an ardent defense of the Czech cause and a not-unworthy sequel to Palacký's *History*. Both author and writings were gratefully adopted by the Czechs, who themselves abandoned the search for a native continuator.[24] The passage of time, bringing new research, a new philosophical climate, and above all new political conditions in Bohemia, made the task increasingly less feasible, and even the position of Historiographer of the kingdom a difficult one. In May, 1876, fol-

[21]   Such is the self-styled multi-authored "continuation of Palacký", *Dějiny Čech a Moravy nové doby* (10 vols.; Prague, 1892-1905), covering the period from 1648 to 1815, by Tomek's pupil, Antonín Rezek, and several lesser collaborators. On Rezek's ambitions to be Palacký's successor, see Jiří Špét, "Rezkův pokus o pokračování v Palackého dějinách", *Časopis společnosti přátel starožitností*, LXVII (1959), 229-232.
[22]   See his memoir, "Vzpomínky a úvahy o Palackém" [Memories and Reflections about Palacký], *Památník 1898*, 158-164.
[23]   See Jaroslav Werstadt, "Dílo a myšlenka Arnošta Denise o dějinách českých" [The Work and Thought of Ernest Denis on Czech History], *Odkazy dějin a dějepisců*, 65-91.
[24]   See the valuable Czech translations by Jindřich Vančura, *Konec samostatnosti české* and *Čechy po Bílé Hoře* (Prague, 1930), in which the French originals of Denis have been corrected and expanded. Czech historians have severely disputed Denis's interpretation of the significance of the battle of White Mountain, however. Like Palacký, he saw the preceding period as one of decline in most spheres of national life and characterized by a struggle for power between weak kings and selfish nobles. Accordingly, he concluded that had the Bohemians won in 1620, the dissension-torn country might subsequently have suffered partition, as in the case of Poland. Absorption by the Habsburgs had at least kept Bohemia intact.

lowing Palacký's death, the latter office simply terminated, and even the title was not given to Gindely and was never used again. The nationality conflict in Bohemia had progressed so far that the Executive Committee did not dare to appoint a new incumbent to the post. In the 1890's, popular and official demands were again made for a continuation of Palacký's history to modern times. The official historical commission appointed to investigate this possibility concluded in 1897 that there was still a serious deficiency of preparatory research. The Estates therefore decided to continue to give their chief support to archival development and to the collection and publication of source materials.[25]

Though Palacký's *History* was not officially continued, his historical working program of archival investigation, publication of source materials, development of the auxiliary sciences, and detailed, critical research formed the basis of subsequent Czech historiography in its rich development after his death. To describe Bohemian (later Czechoslovak) historiography from that day to this is no longer the simple task of chronicling a single line of masters and disciples, but of describing modern "scientific" historiography in all of its specialized ramifications.[26] History ceased to be the province of gentlemen-historians such as Palacký and was thoroughly professionalized and institutionalized. Even Palacký's immediate pupils accepted university posts: both Tomek and Gindely taught Austrian history at Prague University, to be joined

[25] See Borovička, *Zprávy zemského archivu*, IV, 58-60; and Haasz, *Památník 1898*, 543-544.

[26] Bohemian and Czechoslovak historiography after Palacký is surveyed in various fragmentary studies, of which the following are the most useful: George Waskovich, "Historiography: Czechoslovakia", in the *Slavonic Encyclopedia*, ed. Joseph S. Rouček (New York, 1949), 423-428; Josef Pekař, "Dějepisectví, 1848-1898", in *Památník na oslavu padesátiletého panovnického jubilea Jeho Veličenstva císaře a krále Františka Josefa I* (Prague, 1898); Josef Šusta, "Tchécoslovaquie", in *Histoire et historiens depuis cinquante ans: Méthodes, organisation et résultats du travail historique de 1876 à 1926* (2 vols.; Paris, 1927-1928), I, 413-437; Jaroslav Prokeš, "Literatura dějepisná", in *Československá vlastivěda*, X (1931), 254-305 (to *ca.* 1930); Jaroslav Werstadt, "Politické dějepisectví devatenáctého století a jeho čeští představitelé", *ČČH*, XXVI (1920), 1-93 (to *ca.* 1920); Werstadt, *Odkazy dějin a dějepisců* (Prague, 1948) (to *ca.* 1945); Otakar Odložilík, "Clio in Chains: Czech Historiography, 1939-1940", *SR*, XX (1941), 330-337; Odložilík, "Modern Czechoslovak Historiography", *SR*, XXX (1951/1952), 376-392 (to *ca.* 1948); Richard Georg Plaschka, *Von Palacký bis Pekař: Geschichtswissenschaft und National-bewusstsein bei den Tschechen* (Graz-Köln, 1955) (to 1937, with a supplementary chapter by Heinrich Felix Schmid to *ca.* 1955); Joseph S. Rouček and George Waskovich, "The Development of Czechoslovak Historical Writing", in Miloslav Rechcígl, ed., *The Czechoslovak Contribution to World Culture* (The Hague, 1964), 245-257 (Palacký to Masaryk); and *Vingt-cinq ans d'historiographie tchécoslovaque, 1936-1960*, ed. Josef Macek (Prague, 1960), 7-36.

in 1879 by Emler as professor of the auxiliary historical sciences.[27] After the division of the university in 1882, the history departments of the Czech and German halves became the centers for their respective national historiographies (Kalousek became the first professor of Czech history in the Czech half), to be joined after 1918 by Moravian and Slovak counterparts at Masaryk University in Brno and Comenius University in Bratislava. Under the influence of "realism" and "philosophical positivism", Palacký's "Romantic Historiography" gave way to the "Positivistic Historiography" of Jaroslav Goll and his "school". Goll stated its tenets succinctly:

We want to know what was, without regard for any subsidiary or even superior considerations. We study history above all for the sake of history itself. . . . The historian finds only causal connections in history. He cannot determine whether there also exists a teleological nexus within it. Similarly, he himself cannot answer if asked whether history not only advances but also progresses, that is, progresses toward something better.[28]

Goll (1846-1929) had been trained in the rigorous critical method of Georg Waitz at Göttingen. Between 1885 and 1910, as professor of history at the Czech university in Prague, he instilled this method, together with a passion for detailed monographs and a distrust of surveys and philosophies of history, into an illustrious body of students, who in turn dominated Czech historiography until the end of the inter-war period.[29] Among these must be included not only the "Big Four" who succeeded him at Prague – Jaroslav Bidlo (1868-1937), Václav Novotný (1869-1932), Josef Pekař (1870-1937), and Josef Šusta (1874-1945) – but a host of other prominent historians, many of whose works have been mentioned in the notes to this study, especially Zdeněk V. Tobolka (1874-1951), Kamil Krofta (1876-1945), Rudolf Urbánek (1877-1962), Zdeněk Nejedlý (1878-1962), Vlastimil Kybal (1880-1958), Václav Chaloupecký (1882-1951), and František M. Bartoš (b. 1889).

[27] Although Palacký possessed an honorary doctorate of laws and philosophy, and though he was sometimes called "professor", he never taught at any educational institution. The title even caused him some inconvenience: On February 21, 1872, he wrote to Grünhagen, asking him not to address his correspondence to "Professor Palacký". The Prague postal authorities usually sent much mail to his son, a lecturer in geography at Prague University. See Otto Meinardus, "Zu Colmar Grünhagens Gedächtnis", *Zeitschrift des Vereins für Geschichte Schlesiens*, XLVI (1912), 49.
[28] Quoted in Werstadt, *ČČH*, XXVI, 81.
[29] With the advent of the Goll school, wrote Werstadt, Czech historians became *dějezpytci* (historical researchers) rather than *dějepisci* (writers of history). *ČČH*, XXVI, 79.

As a source of national inspiration, the *Dějiny* has served its purpose far beyond the National Revival of the nineteenth century, as recently as World War II. In the fateful year of 1939, Václav Chaloupecký wrote: "The merit of Palacký's *Dějiny* was and is that our nation has not stood without moral support in its most difficult moments, . . . that in a single front with the living nation stood past generations, . . . that at its side stood . . . St. Wenceslas, Přemysl Otakar, Charles, Hus, Chelčický, George of Poděbrady." [30] A lasting literary classic itself, it also exerted great influence on the work of other important creative artists of the Czech cultural awakening, such as the music of Bedřich Smetana and the historical novels of Alois Jirásek.[31] As a model of the early use of the critical historical method, it has not been affected by the passage of time. But, in the light of almost a century of intense modern Czech historiography since Palacký's death, how much of the work is still of scholarly value? Obviously, a good part of it has been amended, supplemented, and superseded by newer research. Indeed, parts of it were already outdated in Palacký's own day, as he himself realized. To determine precisely which sections are defective and to what extent they are no longer valid is another matter, however. A proper evaluation of this nature, requiring an intimate acquaintance with the whole of Czech historical production since Palacký on the period to 1526, is beyond the capabilities of the writer and the scope of this study (Czech research on the Hussite period alone almost defies the summarizing powers of any individual). Some generalizations must suffice.[32]

"No one", wrote Palacký, "knows or feels the imperfections of my work more keenly than I myself. . . . It is deficient on almost every

[30] *DNČ (1939)*, VI, 661; a similar Marxist appreciation is in Machovec, *Husovo učení*, 311.
[31] See the dated evaluation by Jan Voborník, "O působení dějepisných prací Frant. Palackého na novější belletrii českou", *ČČM*, LXXII (1898), 289-307; and Machovec, *Husovo učení*, 313-324.
[32] A new edition of the *Dějiny* in modern Czech, announced as forthcoming in Czechoslovakia, with critical commentary and annotations by Jaroslav Charvát, should provide such an evaluation. I have relied heavily upon the relatively recent analysis by Václav Chaloupecký, "Palackého Dějiny národu českého a jejich význam pro minulost i přitomnost", *DNČ (1939)*, VI, 657-698, in which the author also cites the titles of the most important revisionist studies. Chaloupecký's criticisms are, to be sure, affected by the circumstance that he himself is a pupil of the major revisionist, Josef Pekař. See also Kalousek, *Památník 1898*, 177-232, *passim*. The latest (pre-Marxist) scholarly synthesis of Bohemian history in the period covered by Palacký is the standard multi-volume work, *České dějiny*, ed. Václav Novotný and Kamil Krofta (3 vols. in 16; Prague, 1912-1966). This is a collaborative effort by specialists, extending to 1464, with some gaps.

page." [33] Yet the defects of the *Dějiny* are found chiefly in its broad outlines – in Palacký's prized generalizations and conclusions – rather than in its detailed exposition. Since Palacký was an unusually careful assembler and user of sources, his facts have usually been superseded only in cases where modern specialists have gone considerably deeper than he had the opportunity to do (or into newer, especially non-political areas), or where new sources have been discovered or old ones proved spurious. For example, his reliance on such forgeries as the "Manuscripts", Boček's *Codex diplomaticus Moraviae*, and earlier counterfeits from the thirteenth and fourteenth centuries, seriously impaired the validity of his work on early and medieval Bohemian history, i.e., Volumes I and II. More recent researches have shown that Palacký's idealized picture of the early Slavs as peaceful and egalitarian is false – Slavic society was as violent as that of the contemporary Germans and similarly divided into masters and slaves. That being true, there was no "falling away" from this primitive democracy under the Přemyslids, no "renaissance" in the Hussite period, and no renewed fall under the Jagellonians. It is true that Western influences – especially Christian culture, German law, and feudalism – penetrated into Bohemia, chiefly through German mediation, from the tenth century onward, especially in the twelfth and thirteenth centuries. But these brought about improvements, not decline, in the general lot of the masses, introducing better moral, cultural, and economic conditions and granting to the previously unprivileged hordes of slaves a modicum of freedom as serfs. This gradual improvement continued until it bore fruit in the Hussite movement and was destroyed only by the wars which followed. [34] Hussitism itself (Volume III) is no longer considered entirely Slavic in origin, but at least partially the result of the sudden influx of similar Western currents into Bohemia under Charles IV and the Luxemburgs. Some Czech historians (such as Pekař) see the period as simply another of the periodic resurgences (although an especially intense one) of Czech nationalism which characterized Bohemian history from the

[33] *Dějiny*, I[1], Preface (1848), and V[1], Preface (1864), in *DNČ*, I[1], lii, and V[1], xii. In the 1848 preface (lv-lvi), he chiefly blamed the lack of collected source material and the generally worthless character of the writings of his predecessors.
[34] Palacký was also inclined to view the many conflicts between the Kingdom of Bohemia and the Holy Roman Empire during the Middle Ages as primarily an attempt of the former to emancipate itself from the latter. In fact, the Bohemians regarded the Empire as the embodiment of Christian and Western culture and membership in it as infinitely desirable. They waged a continual struggle to obtain the greatest number of rights and powers within it, enjoying eminent success under such rulers as Přemysl Otakar II and Charles IV.

very beginning and which had reached earlier peaks in the eleventh and thirteenth centuries. Others do not consider it either "modern" or the beginning of the European Reformation, but an essentially medieval phenomenon, one of the numerous lesser "renaissances" and "reformations" that appeared regularly throughout the medieval period. Currently, Czech Marxist historians see it as a deep class conflict hidden under a veil of religious terminology and motives. Nevertheless, although Palacký's overall characterization of the period has been seriously challenged, both Volumes III and IV (on George of Poděbrady, Palacký's "ideal king") have preserved much of their factual validity.[35] The same is true of Volume V, on the Jagellonians. This latter half-century has not been completely reinvestigated or rewritten since Palacký, and his volume remains a basic account.

As the above suggests, much of Palacký's philosophy of history, as well as some of his factual exposition, was rendered untenable by subsequent detailed scholarship. Nevertheless, this did not prevent it from serving as the center of the heated controversy waged by Czech historians over the "smysl českých dějin" (the meaning of Czech history) until the very end of the interwar period. The chief protagonists were the philosopher-statesman, Tomáš G. Masaryk (1850-1937), and one of the most eminent of Czech historians, Josef Pekař.[36] It was at the

[35] Rudolf Urbánek, the eminent Czech authority on George of Poděbrady, recently deceased, claimed that Palacký's idealized picture of this king was still essentially correct, and that Palacký was "intuitively right" even when he overstepped the limits of the sources available to him. *Památník Palackého 1926*, 38-41. Palacký's work on Poděbrady has also had a strong influence upon two recent English-language biographies of the latter: Frederick G. Heymann, *George of Bohemia: King of Heretics* (Princeton, N.J., 1965); and Otakar Odložilík, *The Hussite King: Bohemia in European Affairs, 1440-1471* (New Brunswick, N.J., 1965). Heymann includes many specific criticisms of Palacký's treatment in his footnotes, and both works have excellent bibliographical essays on Poděbradian research since Palacký.

[36] A blow-by-blow-account of their interchange is given in Plaschka, *Von Palacký bis Pekař*, 77-82. Their viewpoints are summarized by Jaroslav Werstadt, "Rozhled po filosofii českých dějin", *Odkazy dějin a dějepisců*, 29-40; and by Jiřina Popelová, *Rozjímání o českých dějinách* (Prague, 1948), a student-level explanation. See also S. Harrison Thomson, "T. G. Masaryk and Czech Historiography", *JCEA*, X (1950), 37-52; and Fischer, *Myšlenka a dílo Františka Palackého*, II, 227-251, 322-345. Werstadt (*ČČH*, XXVI, 87-93) connects the controversy with an anti-positivistic reaction in philosophy and the rise of a "New Pragmatism" which no longer regarded truth as abstract, unchanging, and absolute, but as "a living ideological and moral value" and "a product and instrument of life". He believes it also signalled the beginning of a new period of Czech historiography, replacing the Positivistic period from the beginning of the present century. Prokeš (*Československá vlastivěda*, X, 303-305) suggests something similar when he speaks of "a

same time a conflict between a liberal Protestant and a conservative Catholic and between two disparate viewpoints on the function of the study of history. Masaryk was preoccupied with "historical teleology", with the question of the importance and significance of Czech history for the Czechs themselves and for mankind as a whole. History to him was not merely a series of large and small facts but above all a living legacy, a present and future "obligation" (*povinnost*). Pekař, the "empirico-positivistic historian" and Goll's most faithful disciple, was little interested in the philosophy of history or in its pragmatic contemporary application, but rather in the "scientific" study of the historical development of Bohemia with special reference to its causes and its place in the wider field of European history. Masaryk declared himself Palacký's disciple and essentially accepted Palacký's philosophy of history,[37] especially his mentor's high valuation of the Hussites and the Czech Brethren, whom he linked up with his own day through the National Revival of the nineteenth century. Masaryk regarded the latter period (which he had been led to study in connection with his attack on the "Manuscripts") as a long-delayed continuation of the Czech Reformation of the fifteenth century, and decried any attempt to discover materialistic, rationalistic, or nationalistic strains in it or to seek its roots in the Enlightenment and the French Revolution. Indeed, he saw all of Czech history as essentially motivated by religious ideas (in an ethical, not a confessional sense), especially the humanitarianism (*idea humanitní*) of the Bohemian Brethren. To Masaryk, the "Czech Question" was a universal question and Czech aims those of world democracy. Pekař, in a series of scholarly and polemical writings,[38] rejected the idealistic and romantic interpretation. Like the historians of the Enlightenment period, he saw the fanatic Hussites as "gothic" and denied them any universal significance in European spiritual development. As for the National Revival, he saw no continuity between it and the Hussite Reformation but found its origins in the European-wide

---

transition period" beginning about 1918. The echo of the controversy among other Czech historians is sketched by Fischer, *Myšlenka a dílo*, II, 200-214, 221-227.

[37] His views were developed and made public in a series of six works: *Česká otázka* (1895), *Naše nynější krise* (1895), *Jan Hus, naše obrození a naše reformace* (1895), *Karel Havlíček* (1896), *Otázka sociální* (1898), and *Palackého idea národa českého* (1898). The last work [Palacký's Idea of the Czech Nation] is a convenient summary of Masaryk's understanding of Palacký.

[38] Especially *Žižka a jeho doba* (4 vols.; 1924-1933); *Masarykova česká filosofie* (1912); *Smysl českých dějin* (1929); and "O periodisaci českých dějin", *ČČH*, XXXVIII (1932), 1-11.

Enlightenment and specifically in a new Czech-Catholic rapprochement which took place in Bohemia at the very end of the Counter-Reformation. He denied that the sense of Czech history was religious or moral, recognizing a plurality of factors in its development – general European influences, geography (Bohemia as mediator between West and East), chance, great men, and others. He also rejected the view that the Czech nation had been the carrier of a single idea throughout its history (although he agreed that a basic factor in Czech history had been self-preservation against German pressures), suggesting instead an alternation of "classical" periods characterized by authoritarianism and rationality and "romantic" periods characterized by individualism and emotionalism. The two camps were still sharply divided when new adversaries appeared on the field – the historians of the Third Reich.[39]

It has already been stated that Palacký gave much less attention to the German than to the Czech population in his work. The early efforts of German historians, especially Bohemian German historians, such as Adolf Bachmann, Johann Loserth, Julius Lippert, and Bertold Bretholz, were therefore mainly devoted to correcting this slight and to establishing German influences – cultural, political, and economic – as the primary ones in Bohemia from the earliest times, in the case of Bretholz from the occupation of the area by the Marcomanni and Quadi.[40] In the heightened political tension of the 1930's, however, what had been essentially a scholarly, though certainly heated debate was transformed into a fierce politically-motivated polemic. Sudeten German historians such as Josef Pfitzner became Pekař's eager disciples, deliberately and subtly distorting his criticism of the Palacký-Masaryk interpretation of

[39] While the original Masaryk-Pekař controversy has ceased to be much more than an academic topic in Communist Czechoslovakia, representatives of the two factions still skirmish over it abroad. For example, an American Czechophile, S. Harrison Thomson, writes: "The pendulum had thus, since at least 1912 and essentially since *ca.* 1900, swung steadily but inexorably away from the conservative point of view put forward by Goll and defended so hardly by Pekař to a point where Czech historiography accepted virtually Palacký's view that Czech history was a spiritual pilgrimage in very essence *sui generis*; that though the surrounding Germandom was not without influence upon its course, yet the Slavic kernel of Czech development was so distinctly humanitarian and religious that any suppositious German influence was minor and superficial." (*JCEA*, X, 52.) An Austrian scholar and former Sudeten German, Richard Georg Plaschka, claims that Pekař scored an absolute victory in the polemical war with his opponent. (*Von Palacký bis Pekař*, 79-80.)

[40] See Chaloupecký, *DNČ (1939)*, VI, 694-696. Sample Czech rebuttals: Josef Šusta, "Novy antipalacký", *ČČH*, XIX (1913), 420-445 (*vs.* Bretholz); and Goll, *Posledních padesát let české práce dějepisné* (Prague, 1926), 106-110 (*vs.* Bachmann).

Bohemian history to serve the cause of German propaganda.[41] Under the Nazi occupation (1939-1945), the weight of the attack was shifted directly against Palacký.[42] As early as the 1890's, copies of Palacký's *History* had been burned in the squares of Sudeten German towns. Now his busts and monuments, including the famous Sucharda monument on the Palacký Embankment and the bust by Myslbek over the doorway of his Prague home, were removed, public places renamed, and his writings suppressed or stringently censored. "It would be no contribution to the new Europe", announced State Secretary Karl Hermann Frank in 1941, "for someone to wish to reawaken the ghosts of Palacký's era today . . . with a series of new editions".[43] Not content with removing all material traces of his memory, a long line of Nazi and pro-Nazi historians, publicists, and officials (including such notables as K. Bittner, W. Wostry, E. Winter, and Frank himself), abetted by some younger Czech historians of a Catholic-conservative stripe (especially Zdeněk Kalista and Rudolf Holinka) tilted at his historical and political ideas.[44] Palacký again was described as a fanatical German-ophobe, and his philosophy of Czech history (his *Geschichtsmythos*),

[41] See Jaroslav Werstadt, "Pře se 'sudetoněmeckým' historikem o české myšlení historické a politické a o jeho představitelé", *Odkazy dějin a dějepisců*, 187-213. In reply, in a serialized article in the newspaper *Rudé právo* on the eve of the Second World War ("Palacký a naše doba", July 3-10, 1938), the veteran Czech Communist Bohumír Šmeral used Palacký's words to warn of the danger of German fascism for Czechoslovakia and Europe. It is summarized in Václav Husa, "Šmeralovo hodnocení Palackého výkladu českých dějin", *Zápisky katedry československých dějin a archivního studia*, III (1958), Nos. 1-2, 158-166.

[42] Wrote Eduard Beneš at war's end: "Six years of occupation, six years of concentrated attacks on the conceptions of František Palacký, have only confirmed the correctness of his scholarly and political work." *Sborníček Palackého 1946*, ed. František Hanzelka (Hodslavice, 1946), Dedication. The Nazi attacks on Palacký are detailed by Jaroslav Werstadt, "František Palacký a náš osvobozenský boj", *ČČH*, XLVII (1946), 75-105.

[43] Quoted in Werstadt, *ČČH*, XLVII, 93, n. 4. By this time a new edition of the *Dějiny* had already been rushed into print without censorship (the 15th edition, 1939-1940, ed. Miloslav Novotný). However, a new collection of Palacký's works (the *Dílo*), similarly designed to provide the Czechs with moral support during the Nazi Protectorate, was caught and severely censored. Palacký's political writings were excluded completely; the changes and excisions required in the rest are indicated in the companion brochure by the editor, Jaroslav Charvát, *Censura a dílo Františka Palackého* (Prague, 1945).

[44] In reply to the Nazi attacks on Palacký, Czech scholars in exile prepared a series of articles and addresses in which they defended him and, in turn, drew upon his historico-political thought to explain the Czechoslovak cause to the West. See Otakar Odložilík, "S Palackým za války za hranicemi", *Sborníček Palackého 1946*, 15-19. Wrote Odložilík: "Only the Second World War contributed to the introduction of Palacký's ideas among Anglo-American readers in wider measure."

distorted from a mutual, often beneficial interaction of Slavdom and Germandom into an internecine power struggle, was blamed for having splintered the harmony of Central Europe.[45] Some of his critics, apparently unafraid of using the devil's own arguments, even suggested that the German Reich would become that bulwark against Russia ("Bolshevism") which Palacký had earlier sought in the Habsburg empire.

The restrictions under which Czech historians had to work during the Nazi occupation ended in 1945, only to be replaced by others three years later, when the Communist coup brought about a totally new stage in the development of Czech historiography. Under the Marxists, Palacký's standing has been somewhat ambiguous. To be sure, he has not been ignored, nor denigrated like Masaryk and Pekař. His name – attached to embankments, bridges, streets, and universities – is again omnipresent in Czechoslovakia. The pious annual pilgrimages to Hodslavice and Lobkovice were resumed in 1946 and have continued since then. The anniversaries of his birth and death have been remembered by the popular press and have witnessed the traditional outpouring of publications on many facets of the life of the *Otec národa*, important and petty, public and private. Excerpts from his *Dějiny národu českého* and other writings, fragments of his still unpublished correspondence, and minor manuscripts also have been published.[46] From the late 1950's, the number of these public observances and publications has gradually increased, and the evaluations of Palacký have become increasingly less dogmatic and more sympathetic to him. There has been a growing tendency for the Marxists to see Palacký's political and social "failings" as lamentable but human frailties and as the inescapable result of his "imprisonment" by the conditions of his time and his social class. This "rehabilitation" of Palacký promises to reach a new height during the celebrations of the 170th anniversary of his birth in 1968, for which elaborate preparations have been announced, including a

---

[45] See, for example, Emanuel Vajtauer, "Mythos und Wirklichkeit im Bewusstsein der Tschechen", *Böhmen und Mähren*, VI, Nos. 1-2 (Jan.-Feb., 1945), 14-21, in which the author attacks the *Glashausprodukt* of several national historical myths, including Palacký's. He insists that the epochs of Wenceslas and Adalbert and the colonization period of the last Přemyslids are prouder ones for Bohemia than the Hussite revolution because of their association with the Holy Roman Empire, itself so crucial for the development of European civilization and unity.
[46] The more important of these titles are listed and discussed at appropriate places in the text and notes. See also the two studies by Joseph F. Zacek: "Palacký and the Marxists", *Slavic Review*, XXIV (1965), 297-306; and "Palacký: A Marxist Portrait", in *Czechoslovakia: Past and Present* (The Hague, 1969), I, 594-606.

major scholarly conference at Olomouc and the raising of a statue in Hodslavice.

In evaluating Palacký, many Marxists have relied upon a long-standing distinction, already voiced by Palacký's radical critics in the nineteenth century, between his "good" historical and cultural-organizational activities and his "bad" political ones.[47] Accordingly, his "bourgeois class profile", his political and social views, have been roughly handled. He has been castigated as the liaison between the Czech liberal bourgeoisie and the Bohemian feudal aristocracy and as a counter-revolutionary during the Revolution of 1848. His well-known antipathy to revolution, socialism, communism, and popular democracy – in short, his early nineteenth century liberalism – together with his guarded attitude toward Russia have received none-too-gentle attention. To be sure, he has been granted certain redeeming features. He called attention strikingly to the perennial threat of German aggression against the Czechs, a warning in close accord with current Czechoslovak fears of West German "revanchism".[48] He was a dedicated Slavophile and had great faith in a future "Slavonic" era of liberty and equality, when Slavdom as a whole would be united and a decisive factor in the world. Palacký's defense can also draw upon the high valuations of him by such leading Czech Communist representatives as Klement Gottwald, Jan Šverma, Julius Fučík, and especially Zdeněk Nejedlý. The latter, until his recent death the mentor of Czechoslovak historiography, was for long Palacký's champion, whose repeated praises of him have been parroted regularly by other writers.[49] But above all it is Palacký's historical labors which have redeemed him in Marxist eyes and gained for

[47] More sophisticated Marxist critics reject this distinction, however, insisting that all of Palacký's actions can be systematically explained as stemming from his liberal bourgeois affiliations. See, for example, Kosík, *Česká radikální demokracie*, 89.

[48] See Husa, *Zápisky katedry čsl. dějin*, III, 165.

[49] As early as the 1920's, Nejedlý wrote two articles in which he demonstrated ingeniously how even Palacký's class shortcomings could be excused. He explained that in the early nineteenth century the embryonic Czech bourgeoisie to which Palacký belonged was still a "progressive", "fighting" class; that Palacký considered conflict necessary and salutary for human progress and had made it the core of his philosophy of history; that he opposed revolution on purely a priori grounds but had himself been spurred to political activity only by the Revolution of 1848 and that he had never abandoned the revolutionary journalist, Karel Havlíček; that he considered the "nation" not as an end in itself but as a means of propagating a universal idea, i.e., that his nationalism was a "world nationalism". The two articles, written in 1921 and 1926, have been reprinted together under the title, "František Palacký", in Nejedlý's *O smyslu českých dějin* (Prague, 1952), 144-198.

him the status of one of the great, "progressive" figures in Czech history.[50] Although the Marxists have largely rewritten Czech history according to their familiar formulas,[51] Palacký the historian has come off rather well at their hands. Despite new Marxist methods and emphases, the broad modern historical working program that Palacký initiated and advanced with such great industry remains the basis of contemporary Czechoslovak historiography. The *Dějiny národu českého* is still prized for much of its factual content [52] and especially for the philosophy of history embedded in it. The Marxists are perhaps prone to overstress the role of the philosophy in the actual writing of the historical narrative. Predictably, they are very interested in the stillborn dialectical features of his concept of "polarity", viewing it as a dualism of immutable and eternal polar principles within a changing historical milieu. They value his emphasis on the role of the popular masses in the Hussite movement, the progressive role he assigned the Czech nation for the benefit of humanity, the practical function he assigned to the writing of history. Of course, Czech scholars are "aware" that the *History* and its philosophy were entirely dedicated to providing ideological support for the political and cultural aspirations of the embattled Czech bourgeoisie in the National Revival. But, as one author puts it, "This is . . . a classic example of the fact that a work, because of the value of its insights, sometimes rises above and outgrows the ideo-

---

[50] See the following summary evaluations written in contemporary Czechoslovakia and revealing Marxist influence in varying degrees: Zd. Fiala, "Hodnocení Františka Palackého ve výkladu dějepisu", *Společenské vědy ve škole*, VIII (1953), 237-240; Josef Polišenský, "František Palacký a naše historická věda", *Zprávy Československé historické společnosti*, I (1958), No. 2, 33-38; Milan Machovec, *Husovo učení a význam*, 303-313; Kosík, *Česká radikální demokracie*, 82-99, 426-430, 463-465. Most of the other significant writings on Palacký as historian after 1948 have been concerned with aspects of his philosophy of history and are mentioned and discussed elsewhere in the text and notes.

[51] On the Marxist version of Czech history to 1526, see the provisional official survey, *Přehled československých dějin* (3 vols. in 4; Prague, 1958-1960), I, 7-406, prepared by the Historical Institute of the Czechoslovak Academy of Sciences; *Istoriia Chekhoslovakii* (3 vols.; Moscow, 1956-1960), I, 13-257, prepared by the Slavonic Institute of the Soviet Academy of Sciences; and the two university texts by František Kavka, *Přehled dějin Československa v epoše feudalismu* I. and II. (Prague, 1962, 1959). A brief sketch of the Hussite period in English by the leading Czech Marxist authority on the subject is Josef Macek, *The Hussite Movement in Bohemia* (2nd enl. ed., Prague, 1958).

[52] "The debt which [Czech] historians have to pay to their prototype [Palacký] has not greatly lessened. How much of that imposing pile of paper covered with [their] writings is limited to transcribing and paraphrasing, how much of it contains [their] own personal judgments?" Polišenský, *Zprávy Čsl. hist. společ.*, I, No. 2, p. 34.

logical level of its creator." [53] Thus the work not only succeeded in developing a national consciousness among the Czech bourgeoisie in the nineteenth century but is credited with inspiring all popular revolutionary forces in the nation to the present day. This includes the present Communists, who regard themselves as "the heirs of the great traditions of the Czech nation" and the direct spiritual descendants of the Hussites. Indeed, above all else it is Palacký's high valuation of the revolutionary Hussites in the *Dějiny*, which the Marxists share, that has maintained his place of eminence in Czech history. "We are grateful to the great Palacký only because, with his almost superhuman life's work, he revived the work of Hus", wrote Machovec. "For this alone have the Czech people justly honored Palacký with the title 'Father of the Nation'." [54]

Ultimately, despite their criticisms of their bourgeois forerunner, Czechoslovak Marxist historians have come to agree that Palacký "knew the maximum of truth that a person could know before the origin of Marxist historiography",[55] and have accepted Nejedlý's eulogy of him as "to date our greatest historical genius and one of the greatest of all modern historians".[56] Indeed, with this evaluation practically all of Palacký's successors have agreed, his opponents as well as his disciples. Some of the finest tributes have come from his critics. Jaroslav Goll wrote that "like the names of Gibbon and Macaulay, that of Palacký will always remain a great name in the historical literature of this [nineteenth] century, and Czech [historical literature] will always count it among its classics. Palacký will never be simply somebody's predecessor".[57] Josef Pekař paid the *History* high homage:

The *Dějiny národu českého*, the product of half a century of toil and a work of deep spirit and great erudition, is the greatest learned work in Czech historiography and a classic book of Czech literature of the nineteenth century. Founded broadly on original sources, for the greatest part sources which Palacký himself gathered and discovered in archives and libraries; created in a critical spirit; disciplined by a deep reverence for the truth and many years of practical experience; conceived in a philosophical spirit, striving to comprehend the hidden causes and moving forces of the developments in the life of the nation, and conceived at the same time with that idealistic spirit and morally edifying philosophy which consecrated all of Palacký's

[53] Marie Řepková, "Příspěvek k osvětlení problematiky českého obrození", *Česká literatura*, IX (1961), No. 3, 373.
[54] Machovec, *Husovo učení*, 312.
[55] *Ibid.*, 309.
[56] Nejedlý, *Dějiny národu českého* (2 vols.; Prague, 1949-1955), I, 72.
[57] *ČČH*, IV, 2.

efforts; highly distinguished artistically by the purity of its language, the nobility of its style, and the perfection of its composition – it is a beautiful realization of the dreams which young Palacký had in Pressburg ... to give his nation its history written "according to the ideals of historical art." In large measure it also became that which Palacký further wanted it to be: a great national deed, an aid in the battles of the present, a school of national consciousness and of ideas of progress, right, and truth.[58]

Similar praise from scholars, politicians, and the popular press has greeted the man and his work on each of their many anniversaries since 1876. But perhaps the most perceptive appreciation of all came from the pen of the Czech poetess, Eliška Krásnohorská, in her elegy written on František Palacký's death. She wrote:

"His genius – that was love for his country." [59]

[58] *František Palacký*, 104-105.
[59] "Nad hrobem Palackého", *Osvěta*, VI (1876), 494.

The titles discussed below deal chiefly with Palacký as historian. Titles bearing on the other facets of his life and those of supplementary works which are mentioned in the text and notes are not re-listed here. Titles are usually given in full the first time they appear. After that, they are abbreviated in accordance with the list on pp. xiii-xiv.

PRIMARY SOURCES: UNPUBLISHED

The overwhelming majority of Palacký's manuscripts, correspondence, and personal papers has been located since his death in several Prague repositories: the Archive of the National Museum, the Manuscript Division of the Library of the National Museum, and especially the Literary Archive of the Museum of National Literature. The National Museum, the original legatee of all of Palacký's own holdings, now retains only a few manuscripts of some of his most important (and mostly published) works, such as the *Dějiny* (signature V A 35), *Geschichte von Böhmen* (VI A 19), *Gedenkblätter* (VI A 20), *Předchůdcové husitství v Čechách* (IV A 16), and others. The Literary Archive, however, possesses thirty-one cartons of manuscript materials on all facets of Palacký's life, including numerous additional manuscripts of his scholarly writings (including some significant unpublished ones); correspondence received and sent (drafts, originals, copies); personal documents (e.g., diplomas, certificates, formal announcements, invitations, awards); personal records (e.g., a diary, collections of "thoughts", reading excerpts, lists of authors and book titles, study and research notes, and accounts of archival travels and discoveries); printed and handwritten copies of other authors' works; catalogues of Palacký's library, etc. Much of the correspondence has never been published. It ranges over the period 1819-1876 and involves many important persons, institutions, and municipalities, within and without the Habsburg Empire. Palacký's family correspondence (with his father, brothers, wife, son, and daughter) has been of relatively little importance for this study. Of greater importance is his extensive unpublished correspondence with his employer, the Executive Committee of the Bohemian Estates, and his various publishers. The former is concentrated in the approximately 140 items in the collection entitled "Historiographica" (sign. 11 D 17), covering his appointment and activities as Historiographer of the Bohemian Estates, 1827-1872. The latter consists of his business correspondence with J. G. Calve, A. C. Kronberger, František Řivnáč, Friedrich Tempsky, Gottlieb Haase Söhne, and F. A. Brockhaus. Much more enlightening on Palacký as a working historian is his correspondence with his numerous assistants and with many foreign and domestic scholars. These letters contain clues to Palacký's working habits; professional gossip; discussion of historical issues and sources; exchanges of data, publications, and letters of introduction; and accounts of research discoveries and progress in writing and publishing. Correspondents of special importance here are: Antonín Boček, Józef Chociszewski, Beda Dudík, J. G. Eichhorn, Josef Emler, Karel Jaromír Erben, Anton Gindely, C. Grünhagen, Josef Hammer-Purgstall, Josef Alexander Helfert, Constantin Höfler, Josef Edmund Horký, Josef Freiherr von Hormayr, Jan Petr Jordan, Josef Kalousek, Jernej Kopitar, Louis Leger, Fürst E. Lichnowsky, Waclaw Alexander Maciejowski, Franc Miklosić, Georg Heinrich Pertz, Mikhail Petrovich Pogodin, Franjo Rački, F. L. Rieger, Jan Ritter z Rittersbergu, P. J. Šafařík, Alois Vojtěch Šembera, the counts Franz and Kaspar Sternberg, Heinrich von Sybel, Georges Saint-René Taillandier, Václav Vladivoj Tomek, Anton Virozsil, and Wilhelm Wattenbach. Until very recently, the only index to the Palacký holdings of the Literary Archive was an incomplete, hand-written card catalogue. This has now been superseded by František Bat'ha's comprehensive printed inventory, *Literární pozůstalost číslo 525: Frant. Palacký (1798-1876)* (Prague, 1967). Additional letters to and from Palacký are listed in other indexes published by the Archive. See, for example, *Rossica v Literárním archivu národního muzea* (Prague, 1962), and *Jugoslavica v Literárním archivu národního muzea* (Prague, 1957), both compiled by František Bat'ha.

Primary sources on Palacký of a non-literary nature can be found at various sites in Czechoslovakia. The splendid Museum of Literature, located in a former Premonstratensian monastery at Strahov in Prague, devotes a special room to materials (pictures, facsimiles, busts, publications) illustrating the careers and contemporary historical period of Palacký and Šafařík. The museum established in Palacký's natal cottage in Hodslavice contains little more than photographs, and Lobkovice has only the gravesite of Palacký, his wife, and two children. The remaining five rooms of Palacký's baroque-fronted home in Prague (Palackého ulice čís. 7, Praha I) have been a museum (The Museum of Four Generations) since 1930. It offers some of Palacký's original furniture and other possessions, pictures and portraits, and especially the detailed, intimate knowledge of Palacký family history generously shared by its caretaker, Mr. František Palacký, grand-nephew of the historian. Finally, since 1888 Palacký's personal library has been part of the Museum of the Czech Book in the National Museum, currently located in a former Cistercian monastery and castle in Žd'ár nad Sázavou.

PRIMARY SOURCES: PUBLISHED

Palacký's Correspondence

The publication of Palacký's correspondence was officially entrusted by the Czech Academy to the editorship of Vojtěch J. Nováček. Thus far, however, only two volumes have appeared, covering the years 1812-1826 in incomplete fashion: *Františka Palackého korrespondence a zápisky* [František Palacký's Correspondence and Notes] (3 vols.; Prague, 1898-1911), II-III. A continuation of this series, covering the period 1826-1848, is reported in progress under the editorship of František Hejl. Two other small collections of his letters have been published independently: Karel Stloukal ed., *Rodinné listy Františka Palackého dceři Marii a zeti F. L. Riegrovi* [Domestic Letters of František Palacký to His Daughter Marie and Son-in-law F. L. Rieger] (Prague, 1930); and Věnceslava Bechyňová and Zoe Hauptová eds., *Korespondence Pavla Josefa Šafaříka s Františkem Palackým* [Correspondence of P. J. Šafařík with František Palacký] (Prague, 1961). Selections from the large unpublished remainder have appeared in various periodicals and newspapers and in the correspondence of Palacký's contemporaries. References to most of these are to be found in the bibliographies (see below) of Zíbrt (Vol. II, pp. 802-3, Items 5474-5486) and Klik (p. 64, Item 917). The most extensive of these fragments are listed below:

Bráfová-Riegrová, Libuše, ed. "Z korrespondence Fr. Palackého s chotí jeho Terezií" [From the Correspondence of František Palacký with his Wife Terezie], *Kalendář paní a dívek českých*, XXV (1912), 26-37.

Heidler, Jan, ed., *Příspěvky k listáři Dra. Frant. Lad. Riegra* [Contributions to the Correspondence of Dr. F. L. Rieger] (2 vols.; Prague, 1924-1926), *passim*.

Hübner, Rudolf, ed., *Johann Gustav Droysen Briefwechsel* (2 vols.; Berlin and Leipzig, 1929), II, *passim*.

Navrátil, Boh., ed., "Listy Palackého Bočkovi" [Letters of Palacký to A. Boček], *ČMM*, XXV (1901), 97-132.

"Několik listů Fr. Palackého k prof. J. Purkyňovi" [Several Letters of František Palacký to Prof. J. Purkyně], *ČMM*, LIV (1880), 419-423.

Neumann, A., ed., *Acta et epistolae eruditorum monasterii ordinis S. Augustini Vetero-Brunae* (Brno, 1930), *passim*.

Pošvář, J., ed., "Z listů F. Palackého A. Bočkovi o poměru Čechů a Moravanů" [From the Letters of F. Palacký to A. Boček on the Relationship of Czechs and Moravians], *Rodné zemi* (Brno, 1958), 140-145.

Škorpil, V. V., ed., "Z korrespondence Frant. Palackého s A. V. Šemberou" [From the Correspondence of František Palacký with A. V. Šembera], *ČČM*, CIV (1930), 80-89.

Vrťátko, Ant. Jar., ed., "Dopisy Františka Palackého k Janu Kollárovi" [Letters of František Palacký to Jan Kollár], *ČČM*, LIII (1879), 378-397, 467-481.

Wurmová, Milada, ed., "Neznámé dopisy Františka Palackého: Příspěvek k historiografii" [Unknown Letters of František Palacký (to Petr rytíř Chlumecký, 1825-1863): A Contribution to Historiography], *ČČM*, LXXIII (1954), 322-339.

Zíbrt, Čeněk, ed., "Z dopisů Františka Palackého synu Janovi, 1848-1874" [From the Letters of František Palacký to his son Jan, 1848-1874], *Osvěta*, XXXIX (1909), 41-51, 150-160.

Palacký's Diary

The Nováček collection (Vol. I) also includes Palacký's partial diary from November, 1818, to July, 1863. Actually, entries in the diary (*každodenníček*) become increasingly briefer after 1823 and merely terse memoranda (*zápisky*) after 1827. About one-half of the entries for the period 1842-1876 are not included.

Palacký's Autobiographies

Palacký composed two autobiographies, the first in 1823 (to 1818) and the other in 1864-5 (to 1865). Both have been reprinted several times with minor variations. Perhaps the best versions, and the most recent ones, are those edited by Fr. Krčma and included in the collection *Dílo Františka Palackého* (see below), I, 7-62. On pp. 56-59, Krčma gives a complete history of the previous editions. A fragment of the earlier autobiography was published by Alois Sivek, *Počátkové školních let Františka Palackého, 1807-1815* (Hodslavice, 1958).

Palacký's Works: Bibliographies

The earliest bibliography of Palacký's works was compiled by Josef Kalousek, "Seznam spisův Františka Palackého, kteréž vyšly o sobě" [A List of the Writings of František Palacký Published Independently], for the third edition of the *Dějiny* (Prague, 1876-1878), Vol. I, Pt. I, pp. xlvi-l. It is reprinted in some subsequent editions. The most elaborate listing of all of Palacký's publications, in chronological order from 1816 to 1876, is in the *Jahresbericht der königlichen böhmischen Gesellschaft der Wissenschaften* (Prague, 1877), pp. xliii-lii. It is neither complete nor fully accurate. Palacký's smaller monographs and articles appeared mostly in the periodicals which he edited and in the *Transactions of the Royal Bohemian Society of Sciences*. There is no index to the two German periodicals – the *Monatschrift der Gesellschaft des vaterländischen Museums in Böhmen* (Prague, 1827-1829) and its successor, the *Jahrbücher des böhmischen Museums für Natur- und Länderkunde, Geschichte, Kunst und Literatur* (Prague, 1830-1831). However, their Czech counterpart, the *Časopis společnosti vlastenského museum v Čechách* (Prague, 1827-present), has been indexed for the period of Palacký's lifetime: Václav Schulz ed., *Ukazatel k prvním padesáti ročníkům Časopisa musea království českého, 1827-1876* (Prague, 1877). On Palacký, see pp. 89, 105-106. See also the more elaborate index recently published for this periodical: Pravoslav Kneidl, Mirko Svrček, and Věra Břeňová eds., *Časopis Národního muzea, 1827-1956: Rejstřík 125 ročníků muzejního časopisu* (2 vols.; Prague, 1961-1963), *passim*. As for Palacký's contributions to the *Abhandlungen der königlichen böhmischen Gesellschaft der Wissenschaften*, see Georg Wegner ed., *Generalregister zu den Schriften der königlichen böhmischen Gesellschaft der Wissenschaften, 1784-1884* (Prague, 1884), pp. 64-67.

Palacký's Works: Collections of Smaller Works

Fortunately for the Western scholar, there are four printed collections of Palacký's works, containing a large number of his smaller writings and speeches. Of these, *Radhost* (3 vols.; Prague, 1871-1873), in Czech, and *Gedenkblätter* (Prague, 1874), in German, were edited by Palacký himself. The *Františka Palackého spisy drobné* (3 vols.; Prague, 1898-1902), edited by B. Rieger, V. J. Nováček, and L. Čech, is the most complete collection, with valuable introductions and notes. The *Dílo Františka Palackého* (4 vols.; Prague, 1941), edited by Jaroslav Charvát, is the latest collection. It contains fewer selections than the others, but some of these are not available elsewhere. Submitted to heavy Nazi censorship, it was first released in 1945, supplemented by a small brochure entitled *Censura a dílo Františka Palackého*, which contains the expunged passages. Each of these collections is divided into works literary, philosophical, political, and historical (the latter are in *Radhost*, II; *Spisy drobné*, II; and *Dílo*, III).

Small collections of excerpts from Palacký's various works, including the *History*, have appeared at various times. See, for example, Zd. Kobza ed., *Palackého čítanka* (Prague, 1911); Hugo Traub ed., *František Palacký: Vybrané stati* (Prague, 1924); and Gustav Winter ed., *Myšlenky Františka Palackého* (London, 1942?).

Palacký's Works: The History

Palacký's major work is available in two languages. The earlier, German version, the *Geschichte von Böhmen grösstentheils nach Urkunden und Handschriften*, went through only one edition (5 vols. in 10; Prague, 1836-1867; a reprint is reported in progress). After 1848, Palacký himself lost interest in this version. Consequently, the first three volumes were not revised, nor were the censored sections restored. It is little used by scholars, who generally rely on the Czech version, the *Dějiny národu českého v Čechách a v Moravě* (1st ed.; 5 vols. in 10, Prague, 1848-1867). Perennially popular with the Czechs, this version has gone through fifteen separate editions since 1848 (a new edition is being prepared by the Czechoslovak Academy of Sciences). Of these, two are regularly used by scholars. The classic edition is the "third" (5 vols. in 11; Prague, 1876-1878), a final revision prepared by Palacký himself before his death, with the editorial assistance of Josef Kalousek. It is the last to use the old Czech orthography. Except where otherwise specified, I have used this edition. The latest edition, prepared by Miloslav Novotný (6 vols.; Prague, 1939-1940), is lavishly illustrated and is based on a collation of the "third edition" with Palacký's original manuscripts. Both the Kalousek and Novotný editions have added indexes of persons and places. Palacký himself prepared a précis of his *History* for the first Czech encyclopedia: "Stručný přehled dějin Českých doby starší (až po r. 1526)", in Rieger's *Slovník naučný*, II (1861), 375-388 (reprinted in *Radhost*, II, 487-538; and in *Spisy drobné*, II, 376-413).

Many collections of excerpts from the *History* have been published. The latest, *Z Dějin národu českého* (Prague, 1957), edited by Jaroslav Charvát, is a handy little volume complete with notes and glossary. *Doba Husova*, ed. Václav Novotný (Prague, 1915) is a small collection of excerpts on the Hussite period from Vol. III.

Palacký's Works: Other Historical Writings

Since Palacký's other historical works are discussed at length in the text, they are not separately listed here save those below, in which he describes major segments of his career as an historian:

Literarische Reise nach Italien im J. 1837 zur Aufsuchung von Quellen der böhmischen und mährischen Geschichte (Prague, 1838).
Die Geschichte des Hussitenthums und Prof. Constantin Höfler: Kritische Studien (Prague, 1868). Parts of this have been translated into Czech by F. M. Bartoš, *Obrana husitství* (Prague, 1926).
Zur böhmischen Geschichtschreibung: Aktenmässige Aufschlüsse und Worte der Abwehr (Prague, 1871). Partially paraphrased by J. Emler, "Palacký a české dějepisectví", *Osvěta*, I (1871), 67-75.

Palacký's Works: Reviews

Selected reviews of Palacký's works are listed in the *Památník 1898* (see below), 722-723.

SECONDARY SOURCES

Bibliographies

There are many hundreds of bibliographical entries on Palacký in his various roles as poet, aesthete-philosopher, "national awakener", and statesman, as well as historian. Most of them are of a purely commemorative nature, issued on the anniversaries of Palacký's birth and death and of the publication of his *Dějiny*. Only a relative few have scholarly merit. Titles appearing during Palacký's own lifetime are listed at the end of his biographical entry in Constant von Wurzbach, *Biographisches Lexicon des Kaiserthums Oesterreich*, XXI (Vienna, 1870), 179-193; and in Čeněk Zíbrt, *Bibliographie české historie*, II (Prague 1902), 796-805 (Items 5198-5595, reprinted with some additions from the *Památník 1898*, pp. 711-723). Zíbrt, the oldest scholarly bibliography on Czech history, also contains items which appeared after Palacký's death in 1876, particularly those in connection with the centennial of his birth (1898). An excellent guide to the more recent materials is Josef Klik ed., *Bibliografie vědecké práce o české minulosti za posledních čtyřicet let* (Prague, 1935). This is the index to the works printed and reviewed in the *Czech Historical Journal* [*Český časopis historický*] during the years 1895-1934 (see Items 401, 917, and 2705). Even more detailed is the *Bibliografie české historie*, published from 1905 to 1915 as a supplement to the *Český časopis historický* and since then (covering the years through 1941) separately. A Marxist continuation, the *Bibliografie československé historie*, to-date covers only 1955 to 1964.

Useful Surveys of Historical Writing

Gooch, G. P., *History and Historians in the Nineteenth Century*, 2nd ed. (London and New York, 1952).

Lützow, Francis, *Lectures on the Historians of Bohemia* (London and New York, 1905).

Pekař, Josef, "Dějepisectví, 1848-1898" [Historiography, 1848-1898], in *Památník na oslavu padesatiletého panovnického jubilea Jeho Veličenstva císaře a krále Františka Josefa I* (Prague, 1898).

Plaschka, Richard Georg, *Von Palacký bis Pekař: Geschichtswissenschaft und Nationalbewusstsein bei den Tschechen* (Graz-Köln, 1955).

Prokeš, Jaroslav, "Literatura dějepisná" [Historical Literature], *Československá vlastivěda*, Vol. X: *Osvěta* (Prague, 1931), 254-305.

Rouček, Joseph S., "Czechoslovakia", in *The Development of Historiography*, ed. M. A. Fitzsimons, A. G. Pundt, and C. E. Nowell (Harrisburg, Pa., 1954), 303-311.

Rouček, Joseph S. and George Waskovich, "The Development of Czechoslovak Historiography", in *The Czechoslovak Contribution to World Culture*, ed. Miloslav Rechcígl (The Hague, 1964), 245-257.

Šusta, Josef, *Dějepisectví, jeho vývoj v oblasti vzdělanosti západní ve středověku a době nové* [Historiography, Its Development in the

Sphere of Western Civilization in the Middle Ages and Modern Times], 2nd ed. (Prague, 1946).

Thompson, James Westfall, *A History of Historical Writing* (New York, 1942), 2 vols.

Waskovich ,George, "Historiography: Czechoslovakia", in *Slavonic Encyclopedia*, ed. Joseph S. Rouček (New York, 1949), 423-428.

Werstadt, Jaroslav, *Odkazy dějin a dějepisců* [Legacies of History and Historians] (Prague, 1948).

——, "Politické dějepisectví devatenáctého století a jeho čeští představitelé" [The Political Historiography of the Nineteenth Century and Its Czech Representatives], *ČČH*, XXVI (1920), 1-93.

Useful Histories of Czech Literature

Jakubec, Jan, *Dějiny literatury české* [History of Czech Literature], 2nd ed. (Prague, 1929-1934), 2 vols.

Literatura česká devatenáctého století [Czech Literature of the Nineteenth Century] (Prague, 1902-1907), 3 vols. in 4. See especially: Jan Jakubec, "Mladý Šafařík a Palacký: Boj a vyšší úroveň české literatury" [Young Šafařík and Palacký: The Struggle for a Higher Level of Czech Literature], II, 24-135; and Arne Novák and Josef Pekař, "Frant. Palacký v letech 1823-1848" [František Palacký in the Years 1823-1848], III, 62-130.

Lützow, Francis, *A History of Bohemian Literature* (London, 1907).

Mukařovský, Jan et al., *Dějiny české literatury* (Prague, 1959-1961), 3 vols.

Novák, Jan and Arne, *Přehledné dějiny literatury české*, 4th ed. (Olomouc, 1936-1939).

Novotný, Miloslav, and Albert Pražák, *Písemnictví* [Literature], *Československá vlastivěda*, Vol. VII (Prague, 1933).

Vlček, Jaroslav, *Dějiny české literatury*, 4th ed. (Prague, 1951), 2 vols.

Biographies

All of the extant biographies of Palacký are popular in nature, and only a few are worth consulting at all. The earliest of these is Josef Kalousek's "Nástin životopisu Františka Palackého" [Sketch of a Biography of František Palacký], prepared for the "third edition" of the *Dějiny* (Prague, 1876-1878), Vol. I, Pt. I, pp. ix-xlvi. Václav Chaloupecký's *Fr. Palacký* (Prague, 1912) is a well written and beautifully printed little book, part of the popular Zlatoroh series on great Czech personalities. Václav Řezníček, *Velký Čech: Život, působení a význam Fr. Palackého, otce národa* [A Great Czech: The Life, Work, and

Significance of František Palacký, Father of the Nation] (3rd enl. ed.; Prague, 1912), is a blatant patriotic eulogy. Written mainly to provide "a glowing example for the Czech student body", Karel Kálal's *Palackého mladá léta* [Palacký's Early Years] (Prague, 1925) treats only the period 1798-1827 and dwells sanctimoniously on Palacký's youthful morality and piety. A cross between works analytical and biographical is the small volume by Josef Pekař, *Fr. Palacký* (Prague, 1912). Probably the best single work on Palacký, it is essentially a revised reprint of Pekař's article in the Czech encyclopedia, *Ottův slovník naučný*, XIX (Prague, 1902), 39-71. The most recent attempt at a biography is Milena Jetmarová's *František Palacký* (Prague, 1961), part of the series "Odkazy pokrokových osobností naší minulosti" [Legacies of Progressive Personalities of Our Past]. Half text and half excerpts from Palacký's writings, it too is unsatisfactory. The textual half is superficial, based on published sources alone, and essentially a reprinting of Jetmarová's articles on Palacký's social-political views and his philosophy of history.

Specialized Studies

The following monographs and articles are the most significant for the study of Palacký as historian. Many of them are handily collected in the *Památník na oslavu stých narozenin Františka Palackého* [Album to Commemorate the Centennial of the Birth of František Palacký], ed. V. J. Nováček (Prague, 1898). Two similar commemorative collections were published on later anniversaries, but the articles in them are fewer in number and more popular in nature: *Památník Palackého 1926*, ed. Fr. Konvička (Valašské Meziříčí, 1926); and *Sborníček Palackého 1946*, ed. František Hanzelka (Hodslavice, 1946).

Of greatest value is Josef Fischer's two-volume *Myšlenka a dílo Františka Palackého* [The Thought and Work of František Palacký] (Prague, 1926-1927), an excellent analysis and synthesis of Palacký's historical and political concepts and their philosophical origins, based on an unusually thorough study of his writings, published and unpublished. Written from the viewpoint and with the difficult vocabulary of a professional philosopher, the work has (undeservedly) received relatively little attention from Czech historians. In a preparatory work, a brochure entitled *František Palacký o minulosti pro budoucnost* [František Palacký on the Past for the Future] (Prague, 1926), Fischer has organized illustrative excerpts from Palacký's works under various ideological rubrics.

Next in importance are these basic studies:

Chaloupecký, Václav, "Palackého Dějiny národu českého a jejich význam pro minulost i přitomnost" [Palacký's *History of the Czech Nation* and Its Significance for the Past and Present], in *Dějiny národu českého*, ed. Miloslav Novotný (15th ed.; Prague, 1939-1940), VI, 657-698.

Goll, Jaroslav, "František Palacký", *ČČH*, IV (1898), 211-279.

Jetmarová, Milena, "Palackého filosofie dějin, její geneze a význam" [Palacký's Philosophy of History, Its Genesis and Significance], *Acta universitatis Carolinae, Series philosophica et historica*, No. III (1958), 23-78.

Kalousek, Josef, "O vůdčích myšlenkách v historickém díle Palackého" [On the Leading Ideas in Palacký's Historical Work], *Památník 1898*, 177-232.

Králík, Oldřich, "Palackého božné doby" [Palacký's Deiform Period], in František Kutnar ed., *Tři studie o Františku Palackém (Acta universitatis Palackianae Olomucensis*, Vol. I) (Olomouc, 1949), 43-165.

Machovec, Milan, *Fr. Palacký a česká filosofie* [František Palacký and Czech Philosophy] (*Rozpravy československé akademie věd, Řada společenských věd*, Vol. LXXI, No. 2) (Prague, 1961).

Tobolka, Zdeněk V., *František Palacký jako politik a historik* [František Palacký as Politician and Historian] (Prague, 1898).

Urbánek, Rudolf, "Palacký-Historik" [Palacký as Historian], in *Památník Palackého 1926*, ed. Fr. Konvička (Val. Meziříčí, 1926), 15-42.

Válka, Josef, "La théorie de l'histoire chez F. Palacký", *Sborník prací filosofické fakulty Brněnské university*, 1967, No. 14, pp. 79-100.

The present study is capsulized in Joseph F. Zacek, "Palacký and His History of the Czech Nation", *Journal of Central European Affairs*, XXIII, No. 4 (Jan., 1964), 412-423.

The titles below deal with more limited aspects of Palacký's historical career:

Bartoš, F. M., "Palackého božnost a Komenský" [Palacký's Deiformity and Comenius], *Národní kultura*, IV (1925), 57-70.

Borovička, Josef, "Palacký a naše archivy" [Palacký and Our Archives], *Časopis archivní školy*, II (1924), 1-9.

——, "Palackého italská cesta r. 1837" [Palacký's Trip to Italy in 1837], *ČČH*, XXIV (1918), 165-208.

Čech, Leander, "Palacký a Kant" [Palacký and Kant], *ČMM*, XXII (1898), 105-118, 221-233.

——, "Palacký jako aesthetik" [Palacký as Aesthete], *Památník 1898*, 391-442.

——, "Palacký jako filosof" [Palacký as Philosopher], *Osvěta*, XV (1885), Part II, 1053-1073.

Chaloupecký, Václav, "Palacký v archivu roudnickém" [Palacký in the Roudnice Archive], *ČČH*, XVIII (1912), 332-6.

Dvořák, Rud., "Jak byla posouzena německými učenci vědecká činnost Fr. Palackého" [How German Scholars Have Evaluated František Palacký's Scholarly Work], *ČMM*, XXII (1898), 331-337.

Dvorský, František, "Frant. Palacký a náš nepřítel" [František Palacký and Our Enemy], *Památník 1898*, 443-472.

Fiala, Zd., "Hodnocení Františka Palackého ve výkladu dějepisu" [The Evaluation of František Palacký in the Interpretation of History], *Společenské vědy ve škole*, VIII (1953), 237-240.

Fischer, Josef, "F. Palacký a T. G. Masaryk" [F. Palacký and T. G. Masaryk], *Masarykův sborník*, I (1924-1925), 289-309.

——, "Hegelovské ovzduší v díle F. Palackého" [The Hegelian Atmosphere in Palacký's Work], *Česká mysl*, XXI (1925), 158-173, 200-205.

——, "Palacký a Kant" [Palacký and Kant], *Česka mysl*, XX (1924).

——, "Palacký o vědě a methodě" [Palacký on Science and Method], *Česká mysl*, XVIII (1922).

Goll, Jaroslav, "Palackého programm práce historické" [Palacký's Program of Historical Work], *ČČH*, IV (1898), 1-11.

——, "Palackého *Würdigung*" [Palacký's *Würdigung*], *Památník 1898*, 247-262.

Grünhagen, Colmar, "Fr. Palacký: Ein deutscher Historiker wider Willen", *Preussische Jahrbücher*, XXVIII (1871), 239-247.

Haasz, Jaroslav, "K české historiografii" [To Czech Historiography], *Památník 1898*, 518-544.

Heidler, Jan, "O vlivu hegelismu na filosofii dějin a na politický programm Františka Palackého" [On the Influence of Hegelianism on the Philosophy of History and on the Political Program of František Palacký], *ČČH*, XVII (1911), 1-12, 152-166.

Hostinský, Otakar, "Fr. Palackého esthetické studie, 1816-1821" [Fr.

Palacký's Aesthetic Studies, 1816-1821], *Památník 1898*, 367-390.

Husa, Václav, "Šmeralovo hodnocení Palackého výkladu českých dějin" [Šmeral's Evaluation of Palacký's Interpretation of Czech History], *Zápisky katedry československých dějin a archivního studia*, III (1958), Nos. 1-2, pp. 158-166.

Jetmarová, Milena, "Filosofie Palackého" [Palacký's Philosophy], in Jiřina Popelová-Otáhalová and Karel Kosík, eds., *Filosofie v dějinách českého národa* (Prague, 1958), 135-149.

Jireček, Hermenegild, "Palackého práce o dějinách právních" [Palacký's Work in Legal History], *Památník 1898*, 485-498.

Kameníček, František, "Palackého programm práce historické a Morava" [Palacký's Program of Historical Work and Moravia], *ČČH*, IV (1898), 287-291.

Kohn, Hans, "The Historical Roots of Czech Democracy", in Robert J. Kerner, ed., *Czechoslovakia* (Berkeley and Los Angeles, 1949), 91-105.

Köpl, Karel, "Palacký und die Censur", *Památník 1898*, 646-688.

Kratochvíl, V., "Palackého titul stavovského historiografa a státní rada" [Palacký's Title of Historiographer of the Estates and the State Council], *ČČH*, XVIII (1912), 231-331.

Kristen, Zdeněk, *Za odkazem Františka Palackého: Tři statě z doby nesvobody* [Following the Legacy of František Palacký: Three Articles from the Period of Bondage] (Prague, 1948).

Krofta, Kamil, "Frant. Pubička, předchůdce Palackého v zemském dějepisectví českém" [Frant. Pubička, Palacký's Predecessor in the Historiography of Bohemia], *Časopis společnosti přátel starožitností*, LI-LII (1943/1945), 1-24.

——, "Palacký a Gindely" [Palacký and Gindely], *ČČH*, XVIII (1912), 275-320.

Kutnar, František, "Palackého pojetí společnosti, národa, a státu" [Palacký's Concept of Society, Nation, and State], in Kutnar, ed., *Tři studie*, 7-42.

Lochman, J. M., "Palackého božnost" [Palacký's Deiformity], *Křesťanská revue*, XIV (1947), 298-302.

Ludvíkovský, Jaroslav, "Platonsko-stoický prvek v Palackého idei božnosti" [The Platonic-Stoic Element in Palacký's Idea of Deiformity], *Listy filologické*, LXVIII (1941), 232-241.

Machovec, Milan, "František Palacký", in *Husovo učení a význam v tradici českého národa* (Prague, 1953), 303-313.

—, "Misto filosofie v dějepisném díle Františka Palackého" [The Place of Philosophy in the Historical Work of František Palacký], *Acta universitatis Carolinae, Series philosophica et historica*, No. II (1958), 213-234.

Mareš, František, "O prácech Palackého v archivu Třeboňském" [On Palacký's Work in the Třeboň Archive], *Památník 1898*, 114-125.

Masaryk, T. G., *Palackého idea národa českého* [Palacký's Idea of the Czech Nation] (5th ed., Prague, 1947).

Nejedlý, Zdeněk, "František Palacký", *O smyslu českých dějin* (Prague, 1952), 144-198.

Novák, Mirko, "Palacký filosof a estetik" [Palacký as Philosopher and Aesthete], *Česká mysl*, XXXIV (1938), 227-245.

Patočka, Jan, "Filosofie dějin v Palackého 'Krásovědě' " [The Philosophy of History in Palacký's *Aesthetics*], *Křesťanská revue*, XXIII (1956), 86-91.

—, "Idea božnosti v Palackého 'Krásovědě' " [The Idea of Deiformity in Palacký's *Aesthetics*], *ibid.*, 118-123.

Pekař, Josef, "Palackého titul stavovského historiografa" [Palacký's Title of Historiographer of the Estates], *ČČH*, XXXII (1926), 376-380.

Pešek, J., "Nenavistná kritika Palackého *Würdigung*" [A Spiteful Critique of Palacký's *Würdigung*], *ČČH*, XVIII (1912), 337-340.

Pfitzner, Josef, "Heinrich Luden und František Palacký", *Historische Zeitschrift*, CXLI (1930), 54-96.

Polišenský, Josef, "František Palacký a naše historická věda" [František Palacký and Our Historical Science], *Zprávy Československé historické společnosti*, I (1958), No. 2, 33-38.

Pospíšil, Josef, "Hlavní principy krásovědy Františka Palackého se zřetelem k nauce svatého Tomáše Aquinského" [The Main Principles of František Palacký's Aesthetics, With Regard to the Teachings of Saint Thomas Aquinas), *Hlídka*, III (1898), 350 ff.

Pošvář, Jaroslav, "František Palacký a numismatika" [František Palacký and Numismatics], *Numismatické listy Numismatické společnosti československé*, XII (1957), 83-85.

Potter, Simeon, "Palacký a anglické písemnictví" [Palacký and English Literature], *ČMM*, LIII (1929), 87-141.

Prinz, Friedrich, "František Palacký als Historiograph der böhmischen Stände", *Probleme der böhmischen Geschichte* (Munich, 1964), 84-94.

Rieger, Ladislav, "Poznámky k Palackého filosofii dějin lidstva" [Notes on Palacký's Philosophy of the History of Mankind], in *Zdeňku Nejedlému Československá akademie věd* (Prague, 1953), 437-449).

Špét, Jiří, "Rezkův pokus o pokračování v Palackého dějinách" [Rezek's Attempt to Continue Palacký's *History*], *Časopis společnosti přátel starožitností*, LXVII (1959), 229-232.

Tadra, Ferdinand, "Formuláře středověké, důležitý pramen historický" [Medieval Formularies, An Important Historical Source], *Památník 1898*, 263-268.

Trávníček, Dušan, "Podíl Františka Palackého na vývoji soudobého zeměpisu" [František Palacký's Share in the Development of Contemporary Geography], *Zeměpis ve škole*, I (1954), No. 4, 121-123.

Voborník, Jan, "O působení dějepisných prací Frant. Palackého na novější belletrii českou" [The Influence of František Palacký's Historical Works on Recent Czech Belles-lettres], *ČČM*, LXXII (1898), 289-307.

Vočadlo, Otakar, "English Influences upon Palacký", *Slavonic Review*, III, No. 9 (March, 1925), 547-553.

Volf, Josef, "Palackého dějiny a censura" [Palacký's *History* and the Censorship], *ČČM*, LXXXVII (1913), 157-158.

Werstadt, Jaroslav, "František Palacký a naš osvobozenský boj" [František Palacký and Our Fight for Liberation], *ČČH*, XLVII (1946), 75-105.

——, "The Philosophy of Czech History", *SR*, III, No. 9 (March, 1925), 533-546.

Zacek, Joseph F., "Palacký and the Marxists", *Slavic Review*, XXIV (1965), 297-306. Expanded in "Palacký: A Marxist Portrait", in Miloslav Rechcígl, ed., *Czechoslovakia, Past and Present* (The Hague, 1969), I, 594-606.

Zigel, Theodor, "Palacký jakožto historik slovanského práva" [Palacký as Historian of Slavonic Law], *Památník 1898*, 499-517.

INDEX

Addison, Joseph, 15
Die ältesten Denkmäler der böhmischen Sprache, 72
Aeneas Sylvius, *see* Pius II
Alexander I, 14
America, 40, 70
Aquinas, Thomas, 81
Archiv český, 47
Archives, 7, 9, 35, 38-39, 96, 97, 98, 100; *see also* Palacký, František
Aretino, Leonardo, 64
Arndt, Ernst Moritz, 57
Augsburger Allgemeine Zeitung, 57, 67
Austria, 24, 25, 27, 63, 64, 67, 89; *see also* Habsburg; Holy Roman Empire;
  Vienna
Avars, 84

Bach, Alexander, 22, 58, 95
Bachmann, Adolf, 106
Bacon, Francis, 81, 82
Balbín, Bohuslav, 8, 9, 34
Bartoš, František M., 101
Bartoš Písař, 4, 6, 48
Basel, Council of, 47
Benedikti, Jan, 17, 29, 30, 31
Beneš, Eduard, 107
Bidlo, Jaroslav, 101
Bittner, Konrad, 107
Blahoslav, Jan, 7
Blair, Hugh, 32, 76, 81, 89
Boček, Antonín, 39, 40, 47, 50, 61, 62, 68, 103
Bohemia, Kingdom of, vii, 103, 108; Archive of (*zemský archiv*), 46, 97-98; *desky
  zemské,* 52-53; Estates of, 6, 10, 11, 21, 24, 26, 35, 36, 37, 38, 39, 41, 43, 45,
  46, 47, 51, 55, 56, 57, 58, 59, 60, 64, 66, 93, 94, 95, 97, 100; Executive Com-
  mittee of Estates of, 36, 38, 39, 41, 45, 58, 59, 60, 66, 95, 98, 100; "historic
  rights" of (*Staatsrecht, státní právo*), 10, 24, 27; journals of Museum of, 19-20,
  22, 68, 90; Museum of (Bohemian Museum), 19, 23, 28, 43, 46, 47, 71, 96;
  nobility of, 6, 9-10, 16, 19, 24, 27, 46, 52, 58, 63, 109; *see also* Czechs; Historiographer, of Bohemian Estates; Historiography, Bohemian (Czech); Holy
  Roman Empire; Moravia; Palacký, František; Royal Bohemian Society of
  Sciences
Bohemian Brethren (Czech Brethren, Unity of Czech Brethren, *Unitas fratrum*

G-3